CW01619310

THE
WHISPERS OF THE
SOUL

THE WHISPERS OF THE SOUL

THE DIVINE TALE OF ABDUL MALIK

AN EPIPHANY FOR THE DECONSTRUCTION AND RECONSTRUCTION OF SELF

VICTOR KWESI

PUBLISHED BY

TEBEBA
WE EDIT, DESIGN PUBLISH & PRINT.

THE WHISPERS OF THE SOUL
COPYRIGHT © 2025 BY
VICTOR KWESI

All rights reserved.
Published in Nigeria by
Tebeba Publishing LTD.

ISBN: 978-1-0682686-0-1

This book is sold subjects to the condition that it shall not, by way of trade or otherwise, be lent, resold, hired out, or otherwise circulated in any form of binding or cover other than that in which it is originally published without the author's prior written consent and without a similar condition being imposed on the subsequent purchaser.

The scanning, uploading and distribution of this book via the internet or any other means without the express written permission of the author is illegal and punishable by law. Please purchase only authorized electronic, digital or hardcopy editions and do not encourage electronic piracy of copyrightable materials. Your support of the author's right is appreciated.

Publisher's Contact:
www.tebeba.com | Info@tebeba.com | +2348186808323

If there are no extremes,
Moderation would not exist.
You see, always bless the life of the unhinged man; he holds the key to your sense of sanity.
For without someone being abnormal,
You would not think you are normal.

—

Victor kwesi

Dedication

This book is dedicated to dreamers, wanderers, seekers, and livers of truth, love, and life, whose spirits dance in the realm of chaos and creativity. For nonconformists, transcendent ones, lovers, givers, vessels, nomads, passengers, and performers, this book is a beacon with which to navigate stormy sails.

May its pages serve as a refuge for your restless spirits and a guide on your journey through the deconstruction and reconstruction of yourself. May you find comfort in its words and strength in the knowledge that you are not alone.

This book is a tribute to the warriors who fight against the tide of sameness. It is a tribute to those who dare to challenge their status quo, a tribute to their resilience and courage.

May it inspire you to embrace your uniqueness, celebrate your oddities and eccentricities, reclaim your power to assert your will, believe in yourself, and trust the higher power that guides you.

For all neurodivergent individuals and beautiful souls facing mental differences, to people of colour, and to anyone who believes in their power, no matter where you are in the world, this book is for you.

May it bring you comfort, inspiration, and light as you journey through life's shifting currents, embracing the process of self-reflection, deconstruction, and rebuilding, always in love, with love, and through love.

Contents

Preface

There's a place inside the mind—quiet and hidden—where old memories surface like ripples on still water and unanswered questions echo. Most people never go there. It is too tangled, too loud, and too still.

But some people do not have a choice.

In a psychiatric ward tucked away in West London, where the air is thick with silence and stories, a man speaks in riddles that linger. His name drifts between the rooms like smoke: Abdul Malik. The others call him the apostle. The doctors call him ill.

But there is something about his words—how they land and how they stay. Here, in this ward for people of colour, lives overlap in unexpected ways. Some people are searching. Some are running. Some are trying to remember who they were before the world broke them open.

Malik does not give answers. He asks the kind of questions that unravel you.

And maybe that is the point.

Each voice in this place—no matter how soft, no matter how shattered—carries something worth listening to. Together, they speak of pain and purpose, identity and illusion, madness and meaning.

This is not just a story. It is a mirror.

If you dare to look closely, you might hear something beneath the noise—not loud, not clear, but real—a whisper.

Acknowledgement

To my dear family and friends: your unwavering love, support, and encouragement have been the foundation on which this novel has been built. You have stood by me through my ups and downs and given me strength and faith in myself when I needed it most. Thank you for being my pillars, confidants, and cheerleaders.

To the wonders of nature: Her beauty, wisdom, and boundless inspiration have been my muse on this journey. From the whispering winds to the towering trees, the gentle caress of the sun to the calming embrace of the ocean, you infused every word of this book with your divine essence. Thank you for reminding me of the magic and wonder that surrounds us every day.

To all whose paths I have crossed: Every encounter, fleeting or lasting, has left an indelible impression on my soul. Your stories, struggles, triumphs—each one has enriched my journey and inspired the words that fill these pages. Thank you for sharing your wisdom, your laughter, and your tears with me.

And finally, to myself, for daring to be open and vulnerable, for allowing life to flow through me and express itself through the words written in this timeless work of art. Thank you for starting the path of self-discovery and having the courage to share your truth with the world. May this novel stand as a testament to the power of authenticity, vulnerability, self-expression, and awareness.

With deepest gratitude and love,

VICTOR KWESI!

THE MONOCHROME SIDE OF LIFE

Is the death of another an answered prayer for the hands that make coffins, or are natural disasters a show of ego for nature?

Are tributes an opportunity to free our conscience with words from the guilt of things unsaid and moments not experienced? Or are people being ill an answered prayer for the doctor?

Is a nation at war a divine breakthrough for the man who sells arms, or is an argument a proof of knowledge for the ignorant?

Is an increased crime rate a business opportunity for the policeman, or are broken marriages a blessing for the therapist?

What is value without comparison, or worship without judgement? What are connections without attachments, or sadness without pleasure? What is God without the devil, and what is good without evil? What is the bone without the skin, or a nation without a king?

What is a curse without a blessing, or a difficult time without lessons? What are you without me? What are colours without black? What is false, and what is true? Why are we chained to ideas with locks and keys when life is boundless, limitless, and free?

"What is fire without the cold to crave its warmth, or a melody without silence to give it meaning? Can love exist without the weight of ego, or does it bloom only in the absence of possession? Is life a never-ending thread, or merely the space between two doorways—birth and death? Is grief not love dressed in mourning, a quiet paradox where absence makes the heart fuller, not emptier?"

"What if a mirror is a magnifying glass for my ego, and my true reflection comes to life in the form of my shadow? What if being abnormal is just an act of being above normal, and the meaning of life and its differences is both everything and nothing at once?"

He continued to ask himself, his lips moving slightly, his voice silent, as he calmly paced along the recently renovated ward of the psychiatric partial intensive care unit. The space was immaculate, but cold—a stark contrast to the fragile human lives contained within. The white walls, freshly painted, seemed to absorb the light rather than reflect it, leaving the air thick with a clinical sterility. The hum of the fluorescent lights filled the silence, punctuating the stillness of the room.

The scent of antiseptic lingered, blending with the faint sounds of distant murmurs and the shuffle of slippers on the smooth, polished floor. Around him, patients sat motionless, their gazes locked inward as though the walls were both a barrier and a reflection of their inner turmoil.

Is normal really what is normal? The thought crept into his mind, persistent yet distant. Or is normal just a consequence of collective conditioning? He couldn't help but wonder if the idea of 'normal' was just a shared illusion—the invisible thread that held society's fractured pieces together, masking the deeper uncertainties that no one dared to question. His mind swirled with these questions, each one more tangled than the last. The more he pondered, the heavier the silence felt around him.

The answers seemed elusive, hidden behind the sterile walls, as if the very space was designed to contain his thoughts, not just his body.

Is duality a synonym for the unity of life, or is human discord the synonym of life being just and fair?

Dr. Adetokunbo, known to everyone on the ward as Dr. Ade, moved through the corridor with a purposeful, steady gait. His pressed striped shirt clung perfectly to his frame, betraying a physique honed through discipline—both in his profession and in his personal life. His confident presence, tempered with warmth, often reminded people of a figure from another world—someone with the poise of T'Challa, king of Wakanda, capable of commanding attention without speaking a word.

His right hand rested thoughtfully on his chin, his eyes scanning the ward with an acute focus that only someone with his years of experience could possess. His left arm was tucked beneath his right, resting comfortably as if his very posture was a reflection of the calm resolve within.

Dr. Ade was far more than a skilled psychiatrist—he was a recognised authority in the field of mental health, particularly in trauma and psychopharmacology. His vast knowledge of the intricacies of the mind set him apart, and his expertise had earned him respect not only from his colleagues but also from patients who found solace in his presence.

His clinical training, rooted in the best institutions across West Africa, was enriched with advanced studies in Europe and the United States, where he became well-versed in the latest psychiatric approaches. Yet, what truly set him apart was his ability to merge Western psychiatry with the rich traditions of African healing.

Dr. Ade firmly believed that the healing of the mind could not be separated from the soul and cultural identity. He had spent years developing a methodology that integrated contemporary psychotherapeutic techniques with indigenous practices, earning him a reputation as a pioneer in holistic mental health care. His patients weren't just seen as cases; they were individuals with histories, traumas, and stories that deserved to be understood fully. His empathetic approach, backed by a deep, analytical understanding of neurochemistry and mental disorders, created an environment where both healing and self-discovery were possible.

The atmosphere felt unusually cool and calm for a PICU (Paediatric Intensive Care Unit), a place where children with serious health conditions typically require constant care and attention. Just days ago, three new patients had been admitted, which would usually make the ward as bustling and intense as ever. But it's only 11 a.m., and the stillness seems to suggest the residents had a peaceful night.

The mental health facility, specifically made for people of colour, had a calm yet depressing aura. Situated in a serene area in West London, the building blends Victorian-style architecture with modern features. Vibrant Afrocentric artwork covered the walls to foster a feeling of cultural identity.

The building was surrounded by lush grounds that provided peaceful areas for introspection. The common rooms within were designed to encourage camaraderie and interaction among the residents.

The ward looked different; it had only recently been renovated and furnished after a patient tore up the paintings on the wall by throwing punches at them as if they were hard rocks in an attempt to hurt himself.

But then, the serenity will only last a while before another patient is likely to get up again and repeat the same act. It would be sad indeed to see the new wall portraits ruined—showing the sun casting shadows on the leaves and reflecting in the river side beside the tree.

The painting was so elegant and expensive to hang on the wall of a psychiatric ward. It gave the corridor a very pleasant ambiance and a good mood. For the patients, the ward is a luxurious prison, no matter how beautiful or decorated it is.

"Is everything all right, Doc? You have been talking to yourself for over fifteen minutes and pacing around; you didn't even notice me standing outside my room, watching," said the self-proclaimed apostle of light. "Don't you think you should get the bed next to mine? Don't you think you need rest?" He asked the doctor sarcastically, with a broad grin on his face.

I hope this old man did not hear everything I said. Or does he think his doctor is now showing the same symptoms as him? And why is he staring at me like that? Schizophrenic patients can be creepy, especially this man who calls himself the apostle.

He thinks he knows everything, and the way he calls himself God is just really annoying. Anyway, that's the reason he's here. I just hope I did not speak out loud, Dr. Ade thought to himself.

"Mr. Apostle, you have a good sense of humour," Dr. Ade replied, putting on a plastic smile to dispel the apostle's suspicions and his question.

"Good morning, apostle; how are you today, my dear? I hope you slept well last night." The cheerful nurse from Africa, with nappy hair, thick lips, and dark gums, interrupted their conversation to perform the patient's morning physical examination. Despite being in her late thirties, her elegance made her look much younger.

Doctor Ade watched as the nurse interacted with the apostle. "May I proceed with your morning observations?" she asked the apostle politely, with a reassuring smile on her face. "Of course you may," the apostle replied, as the nurse carried on with the examinations.

"Thank you, my lady; I slept well last night. It was as if I were in my palace in Kemet, where I ruled together with other greats like my friend and brother, Pharaoh Mena. But when I woke up, I was still here in your kingdom where you rule, my African queen," as he affectionately called her, and they both laughed. "I know, right?" she replied. "For a moment, I forgot that you are an African king. One day you will tell me about your kingdom," she said, smiling.

"I am always at your service here in your palace, my queen," said the apostle calmly, as if he were speaking to Cersei Lannister, and as for coffee, I will make myself some after I have taken my morning medication."

"Okie Dokie," the nurse replied as she packed up the infrared thermometer, blood pressure monitor, and pulse oximeter and made her way to the dispensary. "You can pick up your medication in fifteen minutes, okay?"

"Whatever you say, Black Queen, I am always at your service," replied the apostle with a beaming smile on his face.

"It would be nice if we could meet later for a chat; what do you think?" Dr. Ade asked, leaning against the wall of the corridor opposite the spot where the apostle stood.

"Well, that would be after lunch. And you can take the opportunity to tell me what you were thinking as you paced the corridor for over thirty minutes, too."

Hmm, I thought schizophrenic people often forget things. Okay, not schizophrenia; um, yes, dementia. But he was not diagnosed with dementia, just schizophrenia and dissociative identity disorder. Even so, why can't he just get the whole "I am talking to myself" thing over with? Dr. Ade thought curiously to himself, unconsciously squishing his face slightly in discomfort.

At this moment, I do not doubt that he heard everything I said, but I am sure I did not speak aloud... Did I? How would I even know that, when I didn't even notice the old man staring at me for as long as he claimed he did, Dr. Ade continued to ponder.

"Are you all right, Doc?" asked the apostle in a low tone. "Yes, all is well, Apostle." Dr. Ade replied hastily to avoid being caught off guard. "I'll come and have a chat with you right after lunch."

"All right, doctor, I will be in my room," replied the apostle.

"All right," replied the doctor, turning and walking down the corridor.

It had been exactly fifteen minutes, so the apostle made his way down to the dispensary to get his risperidone and sertraline medication.

ENTROPY

A gentle knock disrupted the silence, followed by the creak of the door inching open. The air inside was thick, whether from the warmth or the weight of unspoken thoughts, it was hard to tell. The apostle lay still, his gaze unfocused, as if caught between worlds. Then came the familiar voice, steady and knowing.

"Hey, apostle, you, okay? I hope you ate well and got some rest." Dr. Ade asked, knocking gently on the door to the apostle's room and slightly pushing the door open.

"Hello, "Doc," the apostle replied calmly, slowly rising from the bed where he lay. "You know I would have preferred an African meal, like the ones they always serve me in my palace," he said with a smile. "But the food was still good and healthy.

I liked the watercress soup and the tandoori chicken the best. It's the fourth time I am eating it. Thanks to the people in the kitchen who prepare the food! They make it tasty."

"So, is my room suitable and comfortable enough for today's meeting, or should we go to the common room?" asked the apostle to Dr. Ade.

"Yes, your room is incredibly warm and stuffy, a bit of fresh air cannot hurt." They both laughed out loud and made their way into the garden.

The nurse was a striking Black woman, her skin a rich shade of brown that glowed in the sunlight. Her eyes were deep and dark, with a mischievous glint that could shift from calm to intense in an instant, as though always calculating her next move. Her hair, pulled back into a neat ponytail, emphasized her sharp features and high cheekbones. She carried herself with a confident yet playful energy, often teasing others with a soft smile that hinted at her flirtatious nature.

Her body remained one of the lines of 2Face Idibia's hit song African Queen—a perfect blend of curves and grace that effortlessly commanded attention.

Every movement seemed to flow with the same rhythm and allure that defined the iconic tune, embodying both strength and sensuality. Despite her flirtatious tendencies, she was always alert, never losing focus on her responsibilities as a nurse. Her movements were efficient, her hands steady and practiced, whether adjusting an IV or offering care to a patient.

Beneath her charming exterior was a woman who was serious about her work, always ready to spring into action when needed, yet never missing an opportunity to throw a playful glance or share a light-hearted word.

Her beauty was likened to Catherine in Emily Brontë's Wuthering Heights—untamed, passionate, and wild. There was a rawness to her allure, an almost ethereal quality that seemed to transcend the ordinary, much like Catherine's fierce spirit.

Her presence was commanding yet delicate, striking with a sense of mystery and an intensity that drew people in, much like the iconic character's unforgettable charm.

"I heard your loud laughter from the common room where I was sitting with the other boys," she said. As she walked in the direction where the apostle and Dr. Ade were sitting, the apostle said with a grin, "I didn't know Dr. Ade had a keen sense of humour. "Haha, Dr. Ade, okay," the nurse replied sacrilegiously.

I'd need a PRN when you're done with your cigarette," the apostle said to the nurse. "I have a slight headache, probably because I ate too late."

"Don't worry, dear," the nurse replied, "I'll get you one in a minute." She stubbed out the cigarette on the wall, threw the remains into the garbage can near the garden entrance, and made her way into the apartment and to the dispensary.

"So, tell me, doctor." the apostle asked, looking at him insistently. "What has been bothering you lately? I have been watching you talk to yourself for days; I suppose the conversation must have been so interesting that you lost yourself in it so much that you hardly noticed anything that was going on around you."

"How deep was the rabbit hole you fell into?"

I knew it; he saw me! Dr. Ade thought to himself. Now maybe he thinks I am crazy or something. What does he mean by a rabbit hole anyway? What is the connection between observing how I talk to myself and a rabbit hole? Anyway, his diagnosis was correct. He is schizophrenic.

It is now visible to the blind and loud to the deaf, which is why he told me to come and take the bed next to his. A patient asked his doctor to come and occupy the empty room after his room; he thinks I am crazy. Hmm, how patronising, he thought to himself again in disgust.

"I have no worries," said Dr. Ade, "you know how it is; a man always has something on his mind to think about—just men's stuff, you know.

"Why are you staring at me like that? Did I give you the wrong answer?" Dr. Ade asked. The apostle didn't say a word for a few seconds; he just kept staring, and finally, his lips moved and the words crawled out like a snake crawling out of its hole. "We can sit here and watch the sunset, too. Don't you like being out in nature?" The apostle asked. "Yes, I do," replied Dr. Ade.

This man is annoying. He deliberately turned a deaf ear to what I just said, because he can't admit that he's wasted so much time keeping silent, only to ask me if I like being out in nature, Dr. Ade thought to himself again.

“Here is your medication, Apostle,” called the nurse. She walked up to both of them, her right palm wrapped around the white cup of water, the tablets carefully placed in the medicine cup in her other palm, and she handed it to the apostle.

“If you need anything else, let me know. And if you do not feel like sitting outside anymore, you can come into the lounge. There’s this great episode of ‘The Chase’ on ITV right now, and the African boy in the hot seat is giving the chaser a run for the ultimate prize.”

“That’s very kind of you, my lady. I will come by after my conversation with Dr. Ade.”

“Are you married?” the apostle asked her. “Not yet,” said the member of staff. She answered with a neutral look.

“Do you have children?” “Yes, my sweet little man,” she replied with a beaming smile on her face.

“He turned five yesterday, and his father wasn’t even there to wish him a happy birthday,” she said pityingly, with the corners of her inner eyebrows raised and the corners of her lips drawn down. “We are all looking for love, you know, or maybe you can get me one from your kingdom, being the king that you are,” she said with a smile, staring at the apostle, who was trying to swallow the pill she gave him.

"So, what do you think, Apostle? Are you going to get me one?" she asked. "Even though all men are the same," she said, staring at Dr. Ade, who remained silent and just looked at her.

"That would be truly amazing, my queen," replied the apostle, handing her back the empty cups.

"The aphorism 'all men are the same' that you said earlier sounds like a mantra for broken women, I must say, my lady.

"Love is all around us and first within us, but everyone is trying to find love. Yes, it is a beautiful quest and a wholesome goal to engage in, but if everyone is trying to be the customer, who will be the product? Love is the product that everyone is looking for. If you can be LOVE, maybe you will be found. And you can be 'love' everywhere and anywhere, my Queen," the apostle said. "The right customers are everywhere; just be the right product; like diamonds, be precious but rare."

The nurse could not say a word; she just stared with her eyes wide open, eyebrows slightly raised, and jaw dropped. After remaining silent for 5 seconds, she broke her silence.

"I'm going back to the common room now, Apostle," she said, giving him a smile that tasted like lemons, beautiful on the outside but sour on the inside.

"I will join you in the lounge when I have finished with Dr. Ade," replied the apostle, adjusting his seat and turning to face Dr. Ade.

"No worries," she replied as she turned and walked out of the garden and into the apartment.

"Why did you choose the name "apostle'? Besides, you told me a few days ago that you have no religion, but the name sounds so religious," Dr. Ade asked, staring directly at the self-proclaimed apostle.

"Aren't we all apostles?" He replied slowly to Dr. Ade.

"Hmm, can you shed more light on your question so I can understand it better?" Dr. Ade asked.

"The question is as simple as falling off a log; what don't you understand? Get out your cell phone and search for the word apostle, and tell me what you find. " He commanded.

Is this old, schizophrenic man trying to get inside my head? You should stop calling him that, because if you say it out loud, you know it's an insult and bad practice, Dr. Ade thought to himself as he stared at the apostle.

"Are you talking to yourself again?" the apostle asked, raising an eyebrow.

Dr. Ade flinched, his fingers tightening around his phone like he'd been caught doing something he shouldn't. The device was an old model, its once-shiny edges dulled by years of use, the screen smudged with fingerprints and streaks of dust. A thin crack ran across the top corner, barely noticeable unless the light hit it just right, much like the cracks in Dr. Ade's composure. He forced a chuckle.

"Yeah? Um, no. You told me to get my phone out, right? Okay, let's see."

He dug into his pocket and pulled it out, tapping the screen with more confidence than he felt. His reflection flickered back at him for a second—wide eyes, slightly furrowed brow, lips pressed together like a man deep in thought... or just pretending to be. He swiped, pressed the browser button, and hesitated. Then, as if hoping the internet would save him, he typed: What does the apostle mean?

It was almost funny—him, a doctor, a man of reason, secretly looking for answers like a schoolboy sneaking a peek at the back of the textbook. But that was Dr. Ade for you. Honest, but only when it was convenient.

What he saw astounded him. Damn, why did I hear the word apostle and think of its religious meaning first, forgetting that the word has so many meanings? Dr. Ade pondered with his eyes wide and eyebrows struggling to touch his hairline like a wrestler in a tag team match.

"Are you surprised that there is more to what you already had in your head about the name?" the apostle asked the doctor, staring at him with a witty smile on his face.

"Well, Mr. Apostle, Google says it's the name of an important early Christian teacher or pioneer missionary," replied Dr. Ade, his ego still gasping for air as he tried to prove a point.

“And what do you have to say about that? Because ‘religion’ is written in capital letters in this definition,” Dr. Ade asked mockingly.

“What is a name, Doc? “You recognise the world through the lens of your knowledge.”

“Doctor, does your name define who you are?” asked the apostle.

Dr. Ade, now lured out of the reserve but still trying to keep his balance by not letting his ego hang, replied, “Well, my name defines who I am; it is of Yoruba origin. Adetokunbo means royal, so it defines who I am.”

“But you are not a king, are you? Or you are a king masquerading as a psychologist,” said the apostle, throwing his head back slightly and bursting out laughing.

This old man thinks he’s won. ‘Ah,” be polite. He’s old enough to be your father, and he’s a self-proclaimed God from Africa with no beginning and no end, so maybe he can hear your thoughts, as you have always suspected, and those thoughts you are thinking are offensive, which in your noble profession is also bad. You have a reputation to uphold, so be nice, the doctor again pondered to himself.

Wait, why is he staring at me like that? He asked himself, staring dejectedly at the apostle.

“Is everything all right, Doc? I hope my sense of humour did not offend you, but why the sudden silence?

Oh, I forgot your ego is your better half; you're talking to yourself. Your ego must be quite a conversationalist, engaging so intimately with your mind and always keeping you on your toes. Nonetheless, having conversations with oneself is a profound skill, you know.

But to live truly means to go out of oneself and, at the same time, to be connected with oneself so that one does not lose oneself while being outside oneself," the apostle advised.

"All is well, Apostle," replied Dr. Ade coolly. You have a good sense of humour, you know, and that's amazing."

"My next question is: Do you know why you are here in this facility, with great staff and colleagues?" Dr. Ade asked the apostle.

"You said I had a mental disorder called schizophrenia with dissociative identity disorder; isn't that in your diagnosis?" He turned sharply in his seat, fixing his gaze on Dr. Ade, keeping just enough distance as he demanded the answer.

"Well, according to all the diagnoses and the symptoms we have noted, your ability to see things that are not there, calling yourself God and an apostle, with your constant claims about hell and heaven, the things you share with other residents, the constant claim that you hear voices in your head, your constant withdrawal from everyday activities and your self-isolation, then our diagnosis certainly seems to be correct," Dr. Ade replied.

"So does your diagnosis say that I am mentally ill?" The apostle asked again.

"Well, that's such an extreme thing to say, apostle. The thing is, the signs we discovered were abnormal," Dr. Ade replied.

"What is normal?" asked the apostle. "What does it mean to be sane?"

Is what is normal defined by what the majority considers normal?"

Dr. Ade could not utter a word; he kept a straight face, his arms folded, and his bottom pressed firmly against the chair on which he sat. This old man had just made an astonishing statement. But how do we measure what is normal? Is normal relative or absolute? Hmm, I have never realised the concept of normality so deeply. This man knows something, Dr. Ade thought in amazement.

"Well, I think... Well, I think normal is, um, ahh, I think... Normal is something that meets a standard of what normal should be, and abnormal is something that does not meet that particular standard," Dr. Ade tried to explain as he struggled to find the right words, his head tilted slightly to the side and his eyes looking up.

"What religion do you practise, if I may ask?" asked the apostle.

"I grew up in a Christian home, although at the moment I am still considering which one to join," replied the doctor. "But Apostle, what is the connection between what is normal and my religion?" Why did you want to know about my religion and if I am a Christian?" The doctor asked curiously.

"I had to make sure we were on the same page before I answered your question," the apostle replied. "But you have never answered any of the questions I have asked you," said the doctor."And that is because I have no answer to give you; there are no answers, only points of view, Doctor," replied the apostle.

"All the answers you will need are already within you," said the apostle as he moved his chair closer to the doctor.

The sun was about to kiss the blue-sky goodbye, the wind slowed its dance, the birds made their way to their nests, and the clouds began to lose their colour from white to grey. It was almost 5 pm.

"I have two more hours to spend with you, Apostle, before I go to my office to finish my paperwork and hand it over to the night member of staff, said the doctor."

"That's alright," said the apostle, "experience has shown that the soul can remember quite a lot in two hours."

"What do you mean?" the doctor replied.

"I know that logically and realistically, so much can happen in two hours, but what do you mean by remember?" The doctor asked curiously.

"Well, you can remember the answers to the questions you were looking for that have been occupying your thoughts so much lately," said the apostle, looking at the doctor with a smile on his face.

"How do you know that I have thoughts in my head?" Dr. Ade asked him.

"Because you know you do, but your ego gets in the way. You think you are normal; that's the problem," said the apostle.

"Sure, I am a normal apostle." Dr. Ade quickly responded to the claim.

"How do you know you are not abnormal? You think you are not, and I am, because you have been taught what is or should be normal, and you have evolved to meet that standard," the apostle said. "Doctor, if normal means conforming to a norm, as you've taught, does that mean the Bible is asking its followers to be abnormal by not conforming to the world's patterns?"

The doctor could not say a word. He just stared at the apostle while he was lost in thought about the epiphany he had just experienced.

So, that was the reason why he asked me if I was a Christian. But, come to think of it, is that why people who do not conform to the norm are considered mentally ill? I have read about Jesus in the New Testament of the Christian Bible; he never conformed to the norm, and that's why he was labelled insane and a drunkard. He was not the only one cast in the light; the wise men of old endured the same scrutiny. Is that why my friends think I am crazy when I try to talk about things or ask questions that do not conform, and say that my psychology degree has messed with my head? Indeed, my ego is the veil that obscures the answers I seek. Hmm… profound, he thought to himself.

“So, Apostle, what do you think is normal?” Doctor Ade asked calmly, slowly letting go of his ego and becoming more vulnerable and open like a lotus in mid-July. “You said something very amazing with your analogy. So, in your own words, what do you think is normal, since you said there are no answers, only points of view?”

Defining what is normal is like explaining the term “sweet’ to someone who has no taste buds and the colour blue to someone who cannot see,” he replied. “For the Chinese, eating a certain type of meat is perceived as sweet, but for someone who belongs to a different system, this sweetness about the same food could be disgusting. After all, one man’s meat is another man’s poison. For religious people, it is abnormal to talk about astrology, but in their religion, the star was used as a Google map to show the location of the newborn child, who happens to be the messiah of the same religion.

For Africans, corporal punishment is normal in schools and even at home, but in other systems, it can be labelled as abnormal and even abusive.

Normal, my friend, is systematic, not absolute. Outside a system, the normal becomes abnormal, and reason becomes madness. Therefore, anyone who tries to live or express their life outside the norms, conditions, ideas, and views of the system in which they currently find themselves is perceived as abnormal and insane.

Paradoxically, every day you try to prove that you are normal to others who define normal based on the system they are familiar with. Once caught in the web of inner conflict, trying to be something you're not, the illusory search for happiness through validation and acceptance begins," said the apostle, while staring at the doctor.

The doctor, now chilled to the bone and feeling like Nicodemus, asked, "But how is the search for happiness illusory? What is life if we are not happy? How can we love others happily if we are not happy?"

"Do you want to know? Do you want to go down the rabbit hole?" asked the apostle.

"Well, I think the hunter has become the hunted; the patient is now teaching the psychiatrist; that will be interesting," thought Doctor Ade.

"Yes, I'd love to," replied Dr. Ade, now eager and ready to make the journey and see what a schizophrenic man in his early 80s had to tell him. "Do I need a flashlight? You know holes are dark," said Dr. Ade with a smile.

"No, Doc, you are light enough, so bring yourself along, drop everything that doesn't belong to you, everything you have been taught or told. For this moment, I will be the white rabbit as we travel down this hole. All you need to do is follow me, just like Alice in Wonderland," the apostle said, urging the Doctor to pull his chair closer.

MASS PSYCHOSIS

THE ILLUSORY PURSUIT OF HAPPINESS

"Your conditioning as human beings has always focused on the inadequacy and imperfection of yourselves," the apostle said in a gentle tone. "But why is that?" asked the doctor, who at that moment pulled his chair closer to comply with the apostle's request.

"I'm glad; you seem to be interested in this journey," the apostle said sarcastically, slightly baring his yellow teeth as the ends of his mouth met his ears.

"Are you kidding me now?" asked the doctor, who interpreted the apostle's expression as sarcastic.

"No, I am not; I am excited for you," the apostle said with a smile as he continued.

"This conditioning I speak of is the reason you are always looking for something, always looking for that which will make you feel better, look better, happier, more powerful, more likable, and more perfect.

"You've been made to believe you're sick, poor, ignorant, insignificant, ugly, weak, an outsider, or imperfect, and that you need to be better, with perfection as your goal," the apostle said.

"But that is the reality, Apostle; all that you have mentioned are the real conditions, needs, and deepest longings of men. That is the reality of men," said Doctor Ade.

"You are right, that is the reality of humans; they have made a life out of the words, labels, brands, and profiles given to them by the system they currently live in. It is the same system that creates the antidote that is served to them as a cure for their unhappiness, the same system that they all depend on to create a new reality for themselves, with the antidote that makes existence a utopian reality without pain and full of happiness."

"The bizarre thing is that everyone is searching for the same experience— just dressing it up with different words, ideas, beliefs, and styles to make it feel unique. Oh, how illusory is the pursuit of happiness, the search for an illusory heaven, peace, happiness, and infinite joy!" said the Apostle, leaning forward so that the Doctor could hear him.

"This seed of longing," the apostle said softly, was planted in your mind when you were just a child. It began with something simple—'If only I could have a new toy,' your younger self whispered, "I would feel better.

He paused, his gaze distant. "And so, the idea of love became tangled with that wish, a reward for being good, and a gift for being enough. Every smile, every pat of the head, came with a prize, not for who you were but for what you did."

"That's how the seed took root," he continued. "And each time you were given something for being 'good,' it fed the belief—the idea that worth must be earned, that happiness comes after the prize, and love must look like reward."

"What was once a toy, he said, "grew into other things: approval, success, affection—different names, same hunger." The mind, once pure and whole, slowly became conditioned. Want turned to need, and need became endless."

"You call it growth," he whispered. "But it is just the seed, always reaching."

"The desire shifts," the apostle said slowly, from simple wants to something louder—something dressed up as purpose. 'If I had powers,' the mind whispers, then I'd be happy, fulfilled, and whole.

He glanced at no one in particular, his voice darkening. "Without a fat bank account, I feel like a ghost."

A pause...

"Love becomes currency too," he said. "Since I'm alone, I must be lacking. I chase it like a dying man chases breath. I want it to prove I'm worthy of feeling joy. But I don't give it unless I'm getting something back. Love becomes a transaction—a condition."

He looked down. "I ache for someone to say what I can't tell myself—that I am enough. But I was taught that loving myself is arrogance, so I wait for others to profess it for me. Their words keep me warm."

He exhaled sharply.

"It would please me to bend others into my truth—to press them until they conform, because their resistance makes me feel insecure. And if I call them infidels or unbelievers, it's easier to convince myself I'm right—that my God is pleased when I win people over, and that their salvation is my trophy.

His eyes grew distant. "Sometimes... it feels good to shame others for what I secretly do. I mock their flaws and make memes of their mistakes. People share them. They laugh, I get the followers, and I feel seen. Isn't that what happiness is now—likes, retweets, clouts?"

He shook his head. "A little pill, a line of powder... who knows what kind of happiness might wait behind it?"

His voice grew hollow.

"If I don't belong to a group, a tribe, or a movement, then who am I? Rebellion becomes identity. Identity becomes freedom, and freedom becomes happiness."

He laughed bitterly. “I must be happy because I don’t have a blue tick beside my name. That little symbol, that little—I have convinced myself it means I matter.”

He looked up, tired. “If I run for office, and they call me leader, maybe, I’ll finally feel fulfilled. They say I’ll make them happy. I say if Iwin, I’ll pour happiness into their empty cups.”

“But what I really want...”He stopped. “I want to be one of them—the rich, the admired, the untouchable. That’s the peak, isn’t it—the illusion of happiness built on class, status, and gold.”

The apostle slumped back, shaking his head, disgust brimming in his eyes. “You tell yourself all of this... and more—just to keep the desire alive, and

Dr. Ade watched him, thoughtful. “But maybe that’s the point,” he said. “Maybe this pursuit—this search—gives life meaning.”

The apostle looked at him, eyes tired but sharp. “Aye and it never stops.”

Dr. Ade furrowed his brow. “Why?”

“That,” said the apostle, voice almost a whisper, “is the nature of the mind. You of all people should know that, Doctor. You’re the psychologist.”

“Um, yes, I do, but not in the sense you are making me perceive it now. That’s why I am very interested in finding out why that is— why the constant search for happiness never ends.”

"The mind must be conditioned so that it can give birth to a need from a thought," the apostle continued. "Constantly reinforcing the thought gives it enough energy to transform into a desire or need.".

To do this, the mind must constantly believe the thought, and over time, the thought creates chains of want that turn into an urgent need. Belief is the alchemy, the magic wand that transforms these thoughts into needs.

The question is, are these beliefs organic, or are they driven by the system in which your soul is currently rooted? If they are driven by love, then what is there to want or desire if love is everything and everything is love? But if these thoughts are driven by the system, then residues of the ego are buried within them, no matter how pure its intentions are.

"That is so true, Apostle," replied Dr. Ade. "But why is it so? Why are we entangled in this cycle?" He asked.

"How beautiful your goal, how interesting your striving, how infinite your will, how eternal your suffering! Why do you always desire them? Why are you so needy?" asked the apostle.

"You are looking for this pill, this potion, this medicine, this trend, this affirmation, this saviour, this toy, this title, this label that gives happiness and dampens sadness.

"You try to find it in different things, in different ways. And every day, you convince yourself, using the illusions projected onto you in the form of ideas, beliefs, dogmas, and ego-driven value systems as tools of emotional, physical, mental, and spiritual stimulation and mental self-destruction.

The insanely unfortunate thing is that you spend your existence as a character in this stimulated reality looking for cures, and whatever acts like an antidote, tastes like it, feels like it, looks like it, you kill yourself to own it, worship it, serve it, cling to it and try to be like it. Because that's what sick people do. And who are you, if not a sick person, a sinner, an unbeliever, an ignoramus, the crazy one, as you have been convinced?

And because you have been taught to believe that the one who diagnoses you also has the cure, you rush to the same system that labelled you to find a solution to your supposed illness it convinced you are suffering from," the apostle said as he bent down to pick up the water bottle on the grass. He opened it, took a sip, closed it again, and placed it back where he had found it."

He continued to speak, while Doctor Ade remained silent and stared at him in amazement.

"You keep searching for a pill, a portion, a fix, a new trend, a title, and affirmation. You keep longing for something—anything—that promises happiness and numbs the sadness," said the apostle in a tender and severe tone. "You chase it in different forms, wear it in different masks. Each day, you convince yourself that this time, this thing will be the cure."

He paused, letting the words sink in.

"You use illusions like crutches—beliefs, dogmas, ideologies, ego-fed value systems—each one projected unto you as salvation but weaponised as stimulation and slow self--destruction. You call it freedom, but it's a form of captivity."

He stood up, still staring at Dr. Ade without blinking, voice calm but piercing. "The tragedy is that you live your entire existence like a character inside a grand stimulation, hunting down remedies. Anything that looks, sounds, or feels like healing—you reach for it, as if your life depends on it. You worship it. You serve it. You cling to it. You shape yourself to become it."

He stopped, sat back down, and continued speaking. "That's what the sick do. And you've been told you're sick, haven't you? You've been called a sinner, a nonbeliever, a failure, an outcast, and a madman."

He bent down, picked up a water bottle lying on the ground, unscrewed the cap, took a slow sip, then sealed it and placed it gently back on the ground.

"And because you've been conditioned to trust the one who gave you the diagnosis," he said, you run back to the very system that labeled you, expecting it to save you from the sickness it convinced you you had"

Dr. Ade peered, his eyes fixed on the apostle as if trying to anchor himself in the weight of what was being said.

The apostle continued, softer now but resolute.

"If you believe there's something to cure, then there must be something broken. But what if you're not sick? What if you never were?

"If you believe there is something to cure, then there must be something broken. But what if you're not sick? What if you never were?

He leaned closer to Dr. Ade, as if to whisper very softly. "The antidote you seek is not something you can buy, earn, or become. You already are 'it.' The cure is not external—it's remembrance."

He raised a hand to the sky as if reaching for something beyond form.

"This... this is the awakening—the moment of return. This is the epiphany that calls you to the beginning—to the genesis of being. It takes you to the time before names, genders, jobs, and titles existed. it leads you beyond religion, tribe, and role. it reminds you of who you were before you were fractured by trauma, taking you back to the stillness that existed before the pursuit began."

His voice lowered, laced with fear.

Back then, you were simply an IT, one with universal energy, love, joy, and ultimate intelligence. This was before the personalities, traumas, brokenness, and damages were done, before the shot was fired, and your pursuit of happiness kicked off.

"You were just IT—pure essence. You were one with infinite intelligence, one with love, with joy, with the pulse of universal energy. That first breath you took in form did not require labels. it existed in wholeness. It simply was."

He looked to the sky.

"To remember this is to stop chasing. How can you chase what you already are? Can a soul pursue its shadow? It would only circle itself in vain. To grasp the shadow is to realise it was never separate to begin with."

The apostle turned back to Dr. Ade, eyes glowing with ancient knowledge.

"True enlightenment, he said, is remembrance."

"The moment you remember that you are already happy," the apostle began, the striving end. The hunger, the grasping, and the resistance dissolves. The truth is, when you truly realise that happiness isn't something to be acquired but something you already are, the chase loses its power."

He spoke calmly, each word landing like a soft echo in Dr. Ade's mind.

"This remembrance lifts the veil—the one woven by false beliefs, social conditioning, and inherited expectations. It's the veil that makes you forget who you truly are."

He took a breath, eyes soft with compassion.

"But here's the truth: awakening doesn't introduce you to something new—it reintroduces you to what has already been, and that's the terrifying part for many."

The apostle's voice grew tender, almost mournful.

"Accepting yourself as you are—without masks, without performance—is one of the most difficult things. Nothingness is perhaps the most frightening state of all. And to be yourself in a world designed to shape you—through family, education, religion, and culture, is to constantly swim upstream. These systems mould your perception of who you think you should be and what you believe you must do to be accepted or loved."

He paused, then smiled faintly.

"But remembrance calls you inward. It nudges you down the rabbit hole—into the wonderland within. There, you remember the scary truth: that you are happiness. You are love. You are God. You are the universe itself, playing out life through the form of a character in this grand reality."

"This kind of remembering—this epiphany—only comes when you've released from all that's familiar. It comes when you've let go of the things you never questioned: the beliefs you were told not to doubt, and the stories you've clung to as truth."

He let that linger in silence.

"And when that release happens, the pursuit stops. You cease striving. The truth dawns on you. And that moment of realisation, or remembrance has been called many things—

self-love, enlightenment, awakening, divinity, holiness, salvation, wisdom. The names may differ, but the essence is the same."

Dr. Ade didn't respond. He simply stared, wide-eyed, barely blinking. his soul had been stirred. His heart had remembered something he had long forgotten—something true, something too real to deny.

CHASING CLOUDS

"Is everything all right, Doc?" the apostle asked after his long, sermon-like conversation. "Yes, everything is fine. I was thinking about what you just said.

You looked right through me. Every word you spoke was like a mirror; I saw a reflection of myself in the truth that came out of your mouth. But then, I feel like my mind is in a fog. I worry more and call it thinking.

I feel disconnected and confused, and I call it the tides in the sea of purpose I am swimming in, even though I have been swimming for years and still cannot see the shore.

I need things I do not want; I want things I do not need, and I call it the search for happiness. Every time it seems that I have found happiness, I realise that it was just a mirage.

You said that the realisation of what one is ends the constant search for happiness, which is the root of all suffering, and that this happens through the act of stimulated remembering. What do you mean by that? What is this act of stimulated remembering?

The apostle's lips pursed, and his eyelids stood still for a few seconds. His eyes, sharp yet dull, stared passionately at Doctor Ade.

What's he looking at? I hope he doesn't see through me. This man can be quite quirky, Dr. Ade thought to himself, raising his left eyebrow.

After 40 seconds of not saying a word, the apostle broke his silence.

"You only realise that you have lost something when you remember what you once possessed. You only realise that you are cold when you remember how hot you used to be. You realise you feel dead when you remember how alive you once were. You hate the feeling of letting go in winter when you remember how you possessed things in spring and clung to summer.

Have you not been told by your ancient sages and the little children of the present that knowledge of oneself is the key that unlocks the door to all righteous living, expressions of God, and experiences?

Was it not written in scrolls and spread by the wind in words and sounds that the cause of suffering is ignorance? Have you been paying attention, or have you sunk yourself in convention, stimulating more energy within you to help you forget who you are?

If your holy books tell you that you perish for lack of knowledge, is not the pursuit of knowledge the right pursuit?

The ancient sages said that knowledge is power, but I tell you at this moment that knowledge is only a product of stimulation, and in this stimulation lies true power. Knowledge is only the price of this stimulation, and this stimulation is curiosity because, without curiosity, knowledge is only a noun, which in its true nature is a verb.

In your school system, you are graded on an exam according to how much information you can remember. Your ability to remember is a prerequisite for the assessment of your knowledge in the tested subject area.

The same logic applies to the universe. The degree of self-knowledge depends on how much of who you are you can remember in every passing moment. This knowledge, therefore, influences your decisions at that moment.

So, your question, doctor, should be: How much of myself have I forgotten? What decisions have I made that have encouraged forgetting rather than remembering? Every decision made at all times stimulates each of these actions: an ego-driven action that stimulates forgetting or a love-driven action that stimulates remembering."

Doctor Ade took a deep breath, his right elbow resting on his thigh and his right palm gently stroking his jaw as he glanced firmly at the apostle.

“Honestly, Apostle, this is deep,” he said. “The desire to become a psychologist stemmed from my hunger for an answer to the big question of who I am. The reason I am not getting answers yet might be because I have been asking the wrong questions”.

“Nothing in the universe can tell what a creation is, what constitutes its essence, value, and purpose, without the help of a mirror. There must be a standard by which to examine.

The only mirrors that exist and that express the true reflection of all things in the universe are knowledge of the creation and that of the creator,” the apostle replied slowly.

“So, you mean that if I want to know who I am, I have to know who my creator is, and to know who my creator is, I have to know who I am?” asked the doctor.

“Do you remember how your phone rang when my African queen came to give me my medication?” asked the apostle with a grin.

“Who is your African queen? Oh, you mean the female member of staff? Yes, my phone rang,” Dr. Ade replied hastily. “But what does your ‘African queen’ or my ‘phone ringing’ have to do with the question I just asked?”

The apostle smiled slowly. “Therein lies your answer,” he said.

What is this man saying? Maybe he's having a schizophrenic episode, and I don't even know. The doctor thought to himself.

"I still do not understand what you mean, Apostle," said the doctor.

"How did she know who the singer was when the phone rang and the ringtone started playing?" asked the apostle

"Probably because she recognised the singer's voice," replied Doctor Ade.

"By what has been created, she has recognised who the Creator is," the apostle replied. "I hope you have got your answer now?"

"Well... I think so," said Doctor Ade, who paused and suddenly began to smile. "So, you are just saying that I need to know who my creator is to understand myself. Well, my creator is God, and I understand him to be the creator of heaven and earth."

"When you say God, what do you mean?" asked the apostle with his head tilted slightly to one side, his eyes darkened, his right hand to his lips, his elbow resting on his thigh, and his back leaning forward.

"What is confusing about it? The name of God is self-explanatory. God in the sense of Creator of all things, Allah in Islam—that's what I mean when I say God," replied Dr. Ade boldly.

"You say you understand him to be the creator of heaven and earth; is this God male?" The apostle asked.

“Well, as far as I know, His name is God, but as for the pronoun or gender, I really do not know what to say,” Doctor Ade replied with his head slightly bowed and an inhibited smile on his face.

“Do you believe in your idea of God because you think it is true, or do you believe because the name and the gender are most familiar to you?” The apostle asked.

“A man who has grown up in a family that believes in self-realisation through the laws of Islam is right in his definition and understanding of God as Allah, the Supreme Being; he is familiar with it. But if, by your definition, he is the one true God and the creator of heaven and earth, then that should include trees and animals, right?”

“Yes, of course,” replied Dr. Ade. “The real question is whether the tree recognises the being by the names of God or Allah, as man does through various religious beliefs,” said the apostle. “But animals, like trees, do not speak and have no consciousness like humans,” Dr. Ade hastily replied.

The apostle stared at him, shook his head indignantly, and said, “Do not give your ego the space to argue with your soul by telling yourself that animals and trees have no consciousness, because all living beings have life in them that expresses and experiences itself as it is in you.

You will say: Yes, I have experienced him. He is called God. He has done things that are wonderful in my eyes, and his magnanimity is so great that no human being can compare with it.

Others, too, who have different religious practices from those with which you are familiar, have had their experiences in their way. Various souls have experienced them through the study of the moon, the sun, images, ideas, their ancestors, fairy tales, symbols, numbers, trees, animals, and women. The path the soul takes that leads to this divine experience determines the soul's perception of God. And whatever the soul's perception is, it is right and true.

This divine, formless, and nameless experience forms an identity so that the mind can make sense of it and express itself effectively through the body. Aye, how well can one best identify a thing if it is not limited by labels and names?

The trees are not English, so they don't recognise this experience as God, and neither do the animals. Yet, it is a miracle to watch the swan glide effortlessly across the water, suddenly overcoming gravity as it flaps its white wings, lands on the shore of the lake, and walks on the same water it just sailed over. It takes a miracle for a tiny seed like an acorn to become an oak tree or an egg to transform into a butterfly.

So, what makes the definition of your own divine experience and the name you give it so profound? What makes the belief that its name is God, Allah, or any other name from the religion you practise so special?

Verily, its name and gender are based on the momentary experience and expression of itself, since it expresses itself through the vessels you come into contact with at every moment.

Therefore, your expression at every moment with everything it has created is an expression of it, and when you are fully aware of this, it tells you who or what it is, or what its name and gender are at that very moment," the apostle said calmly.

"So, after all you have heard now, what do you think his name is?" the apostle asked Doctor Ade.

This man is trying to confuse my mind. Since I am experiencing him at this moment, and he has life in him, he is a vessel through which life experiences itself. If my Christian upbringing shapes my view of life as a reflection of the divine, then I can't help but wonder. Does that not make Him God, or perhaps the echo of Himself in the vastness of existence?

Um, that can't be. God can't be schizophrenic. This man is just trying to confuse my mind. He must have lost his mind. Well, that's why he's here in the first place, Dr. Ade wondered, raising his eyebrows curiously.

"Um, are you saying that, at this moment, according to what you've said, the name of God is Apostle because I am the one who is experiencing you as life expresses itself through you?" Doctor Ade asked the apostle.

"I am an insane person, and you are my physician. Its name is on your lips, and its root is buried in your heart. The experience is yours; the naming and defining is therefore your task," replied the apostle.

"When you are hungry and pray to it, asking it for your daily bread by the words and methods of any practice you believe in, and it provides a sheep for you to slaughter and enjoy, in that moment, its name is the name of the sheep. It expresses itself in the form of a sheep, so that your hunger is satisfied and your prayers are answered.

For the farmer, his name becomes rain when he prays for growth. For the lion, its name becomes the name of the animal that life gives it to hunt.

It dwells in all things because it is all things; it is in all things; it is outside all things. Your perception is based on the vulnerability of your soul, the emptiness of your mind, and the nakedness of your heart.

"Do you observe things just to look at them, or do you truly see them to understand? Do you perceive things only to love and admire them, or do you perceive them only to judge and compare? When you love something, you see it as it truly is in every moment. When you adore it, you connect with its soul, where inner standing resides. Only then can you feel that which you call God, Allah, Universal Intelligence, Chi, or whatever you want to call it, in all things you experience and express.

Your full awareness of this being, experience, or source leads to your inner awareness. This inner understanding sparks curiosity, he continued. It drives you to ask questions. And every act of questioning, every desire to seek, creates an inner deconstruction that gradually removes the ideas, concepts, and conditioning that cloud your consciousness, suppress your inner child, and make you forget who you are," the apostle said.

"That's the reason for my problem," explained Dr. Ade. "Because I have read books, and I am well aware of the part of the Christian Bible that says God is in me. Well, God is within me, and I say God because I grew up with Christian values and ideas of what or who God is. But in truth, I have questions that I have always asked and still have not gotten answers to.

I have consulted spiritual minds and read spiritual books written by the best authors, sages, and prophets, and I have even gone so far as to delve into religious practices out of curiosity just to find an answer to my biggest questions: Who am I? Is there a God? How can I recognise him in myself and others?" Doctor Ade asked.

"What have you been taught about God in your Christian practice?" asked the apostle.

"I was taught that God is a being in the third heaven. This heaven and all that is in it are made of gold. He sits on a golden throne, and the angels are all dressed in white, with great white wings, singing without ceasing. The twelve elders sit beside the throne, and Jesus sits at the right hand of the Father. There is also an angel with a great trumpet ready to blow, and as soon as he does, the Rapture will take place. But Jesus has asked his Father for more time so that everyone can repent before the angel blows the trumpet.

"A truly fascinating story," exclaimed the apostle, raising eyebrows and giving him a round of applause.

"That's not all," continued Doctor Ade, "I was also taught about the devil. He was thrown into the abyss by God, where he reigns with his demons."

"They could be right because this story sounds so real and true. Then, what is God to you? What is your view? How do you see him?" the apostle asked.

"To be honest, apostle, I have not found an answer to this question. Why do you think I said I abandoned Christian perspectives out of curiosity? I started questioning all those noble ideals, values, and stories that I had been taught since childhood in the Christian family I was raised in. And you know how painful the act of unlearning can be," Dr. Ade replied.

"Whenever I feel like I have found the right words or the right meaning for the question, they change it. Just a few minutes ago, you changed what I thought was the right meaning. You and I are God in every moment of life in which we express and experience ourselves. Because, as you say, God is both the expresser, the experience, and the expression.

I used to think that if I did not believe in all these stories told to me by all these systems, if I was spiritually rebellious, then I could find the meaning my soul was looking for. But the more rebellious I am, the more I conform to what I am running away from.

I thought that by discovering spirituality, I had found freedom. Yes, it has changed my view of God from something outside of me to something inside of me, but I am still not fulfilled. So, I agree with everything you said earlier. But I still have questions, Apostle," Dr. Ade asked.

"What does your soul want to remember, Doc?" asked the apostle.

"My question is," Dr. Ade continued. "When it comes to religion, while I do not agree with the things that are preached, taught, and proclaimed today in the name of God, I do agree with the teachings of Jesus in Christianity about love and self-knowledge. I also like the teachings of the Prophet Mohammed in Islam about the Oneness of God, his insistence on total faith in Allah. There is some truth in that.

Not to forget the teachings of Lord Krishna, who said that truth and dharma would lead you to the path of righteousness, and his views on the law of karma. I also respect the teachings of the Buddha, like the three universal truths, the four noble truths, and the noble eightfold path. I believe in these teachings because, logically and realistically, they are all food for the soul. So, which is the ultimate truth if all these religions claim to be the truth?" Dr. Ade asked, shrugging his shoulders, remaining silent, and waiting for the apostle to speak.

"There is truth in all things, but one must be aware of the truth to recognise and experience it. You cannot try to remember something you are not aware of. Awareness makes searching easy; it helps you recognise the truth when you encounter it. This way, you do not constantly seek and find nothing," replied the apostle.

"But I hate religion," said Dr. Ade abruptly. "I don't want to sound atheistic; don't get me wrong, but I am trying to unlearn everything I have learned about the religious God. As a thinking person, I have found so many inconsistencies that I just cannot accept," Dr. Ade said with a slightly raised tone.

"As for the truth that's in all these texts, I can't say it or agree with it completely, but some of the things they say are true on a common-sense level. However, religion doesn't lead you to God, and I am very sure of that. But if it does, then there must be something wrong with their God. I cannot wrap my head around the idea of a God who would be so transactional and conditional in all his actions. Every war waged by humans is waged in their name. He watches people who love him perish. Yes, they would say, it is not him. But then, why can't he stop the killing? Do you have to accept His son as your saviour in order to be saved?"

"Does he hate the black skin so much that everything about him is white? It's obvious he hates black people, too. They cannot go through all they have been through for over four hundred years, and all he could do was remain mute.

To make matters worse, the angels have Western names, their clothes are always white, and there are more Western saints than even African ones. Why does he hate women so much that he makes it seem as if women are the gateway through which sin entered the world, like the temptation of Eve by the serpent in the Garden of Eden?

Not to mention that religion has portrayed women as if they were the end of great men. Samson, the strongest man in the world, was robbed of his strength because he was susceptible to love and elegance. Shouldn't his openness and vulnerability to love and elegance increase his strength? Why was it the end of his strength? There are just too many inconsistencies.

Frankly, it does not make sense to me. So, Apostle, when I say I do not like religion, I mean it. The thing is, I am currently opting for spirituality, and its idea of God makes more sense to me, to be fair.

I also appreciate African spirituality; I embrace it because it takes me back to my roots as a black man. Africa is the cradle of all spirituality," Dr Ade asserted convincingly, while the apostle remained silent, staring at him as he continued speaking.

"I know that people are too conditioned to see this light, that the root of all spirituality is Africa. But for me, it helped me realise that the Christianity I grew up with was just brainwashing.

I realised that Jesus was a black man, so why did they make him white? The stories in the Bible were stolen from the Egyptian Book of the Dead. How can a white man die for my sins? We all know that's not possible if they can't even share their land with me.

The truth is, apostle, I can talk about all this as much as I want, but deep down, something is missing. What if my ancestors had also practised African spirituality based on conventional thinking? What if they had practised it simply because it was the only thing they knew, and accepting a foreign belief system was a consequence of the new knowledge they gained?

Also, they had to learn to read and write to read the Bible, which became the tool for their conditioning. Reading and writing are forms of self-expression, which is not a terrible thing to learn.

What if the fact that Jesus is black and not white is just another conventional notion that our black ancestors popularised and labelled as truth over time? What if the figure of Jesus is just an idea that serves to represent one's higher self, and the question of his skin colour and race only serves to distract people, creating arguments and division?

But anyway, now that you have heard my gibberish," said Dr Ade sarcastically, "can you tell me something about your idea of God?

What or who do you think God is?" Dr Ade asked, glancing at his wristwatch. "We still have an hour, so there is time to listen to your answer."

TORN VEIL

"you have searched, rebelled, questioned, and discovered what God is not—yet have you recognised what God is?"

How can you know yourself when you are fighting against yourself? Were you not taught that understanding is the fruit of love? Can love live in the house that War built? Two cannot walk together if they do not agree. Harmony between the self you imagine and the self you truly are is impossible if there is no cohesion between the two," said the apostle.

"Everything you've said reflects what different religions, people, and scholars—living and dead—believe about God and their experience of a supreme being." Even the spirituality of your ancestors, whose beliefs you now place far above all religions, is just ideas that come from their experiences with the idea of God and the supreme consciousness.

How I see God is meaningless if you want to cling to my experience as the ultimate truth. All experiences of God, love, life, and their expressions in all created things are individualistic.

Salvation, your prophets proclaim, is a personal journey. Therefore, I tell you, as I told your ancestors, that all the experiences, ideas, expressions, beliefs, and teachings of others are flashlights for you to use on your path to self-knowledge. But what good is a flashlight in the sunlight? It is useless to beg for a cup of water when you have streams of living water flowing within you.

Why will you not be incessantly thirsty if you have made it your life's work to evaluate, judge, and compare hard water, soft water, spring water, grey water, rainwater, and distilled water?

Is it the water you seek to quench your thirst, or the illusion of freedom that rebellion offers a mind full of knowledge but lacking understanding? If it is the water you seek, shouldn't you realise that everything you compare shares the same essence, and that names, titles, and teachings are mere labels shaped by personal experience of beauty in diversity?

The time and energy that should have been invested in worship and love, you have instead spent on comparison and judgment.

What is the yardstick for your comparisons? What is the basis for your judgement? Why do you look for God, his experience, and expression in the ideas of others when you have not found him within yourself? Why do you seek the light in another's torch when you are blind to the sunlight within you? Why seek love in the heart of another when you have not found it in your own heart?

It takes more energy to judge than to love. No wonder you are always thirsty, thinking that seeking God will quench your thirst. Can you find something that is not lost? You think God is lost, so your goal in life is to find Him. But you can only become fully aware of His omnipresence, within you and around you, the moment you love, for when you love, all searching stops.

What is love, then, if not universal intelligence, the will to create, the joy of expressing oneself, the vulnerability to evolve, and the courage to experience the painful joy of feeling? What is God if not the energy that creates, expresses, and experiences, constantly driving the soul to feel?

When you experience, feel, and express yourselves, God also feels, expresses, and experiences. You are God playing a human character in this play of existence, in form, for the sole purpose of experiencing and expressing self. Just as it also plays animal and plant characters, all of nature serves as props in the same play of existence."

Dr. Ade just stared at him; he could not say a word.

How does this man know all this? Is schizophrenia linked to a deep understanding of life? He asked himself.

Finally, he broke his silence with a question. "So, when you say that God acts simultaneously in all things, what do you mean?"

The apostle paused for 7 seconds, as if counting his breath, and began to speak again.

"In your house, the same energy in a fuse box powers all the appliances simultaneously. Each appliance operates at the level it can handle and the energy it needs. The TV works as a TV, the microwave works as a microwave, and the fridge works as a fridge, all at the same time. Any appliance in the house that cannot be powered by the energy from the fuse box is either faulty or has not been switched on for the energy to reach it.

In the same way, divine energy powers all things that are aware of its presence, that are alive, loving, vulnerable, and open. It expresses itself through the nature of whatever it powers, be it a human, animal, or plant, in every moment of existence."

"That's so much to take in at once, but I will take my time and digest it all," Dr. Ade replied with a smile as he brushed off a beetle perched on his right thigh.

"Your sages and prophets have taught you that God is love," continued the apostle. "I tell you, Doctor, as I told your fathers and their ancestors, that God is both the ego and love. One is the substance, and the other is its shadow. But both are from the same source: life. To be godly is to live in love, and to be righteous is to love freely.

You love when you create, when you express life, and when you are open enough to experience life and to feel it as it is, without judgment, comparisons, or definitions. You love when you are vulnerable enough to change, because openness to change is the root of non-attachment. In non-attachment, love thrives majestically, ever young, wild, and free. And in this freedom, you experience and express God without seeking or trying to find him in others' words, ideas, or religious beliefs.

Truly, love is too great to be conditioned and categorised, Doc. Life is too nameless to be named. God is too divine to be boxed and personified. Religion, no matter how intense the light it spreads, can be no brighter than the sun. The torch has its use when God is at rest, but when the sun rises, the torch must be extinguished."

"Once again, I will take time to digest this," Doctor Ade replied hastily, just as the apostle dropped his last sentence on his ear. "I understand every word you said, but I still need clarity on something you mentioned that I think is profound. Go on, what is it that you need clarity on?" the apostle asked.

"Well, if God is love, as you said, and you've also compared him to the sun—which now helps me understand who God is—then who am I?" Dr Ade asked.

"As you pray amiss, so you ask amiss," the apostle replied. If you don't know yourself, how can a schizophrenic old man with a personality disorder know you?" "How can you know if the description I give of you is really who you are? How can a blind man tell another blind man what the colour purple looks like? Don't you know that his answer will be based on what he has heard from others because he does not know what purple is or what it looks like?

The people, teachings, laws, and ideas you rely on—whether from communities, books, or spiritual leaders—can only describe you by the standards their systems gave them. No one can truly know or define who you are except yourself.

If you are made in the image and likeness of energy, what are you but energy? If the breath of life lives rent-free in your lungs, what are you but life itself? That which you call yourself is just the character through which life expresses itself in this play of existence and through which it experiences itself.

For the character to connect with and function in existence, it must be temporarily conditioned either by its soul or the body, with your power of choice buried in your mind as the whip of conditioning. Every choice you make is a mirror in which you can instantly perceive yourself. When you examine your choices with full awareness, you will see who and what you truly are."

"I think we will stop for today, doctor. Tranquilly has sent messages through the wind that has just blown by. It is an honour to nature to answer when she calls," said the apostle, slowly rising from his seat.

"Lest I forget, I was told earlier this week that there will be a group therapy event on the ward this week. How true is this information?"

"Umm, it's not group therapy per se. Tomorrow is Friday, and the occupational therapist has made food and snacks for everyone so that they can chat and socialise. Also, the boys on the ward wanted to hear you speak," replied Dr. Ade with a grin.

Hear me speak? "Now you're teasing me," a schizophrenic like me, the apostle replied with a laugh, patting Dr. Ade on the shoulder as they both made their way to the door leading to the corridor. The apostle walked slowly ahead, while Dr. Ade walked behind him.

Is this man schizophrenic, or is he really what he claims to be? Dr. Ade wondered as they both entered the apartment.

"Thank you for the words," Dr. Ade said from behind the apostle as they made their way into the building. "It was exciting to listen to your truth; it was so enlightening."

"Well, words only fulfil their purpose only when used as intended. That is, they are a torch that helps one see clearly what is not and to remember what is.

All the words that came out of my mouth as we sat in the company of flowers, the evening sky, the cool wind, and the green grasses that listened, even though we trampled on them for hours, are just a fork in the road that leads to the divine remembering of who you are.

"So, what you have heard can only be perceived as truth if it helps you to revive what is dead and buried in you, suffocated by the ego, driven by fear, ideas, dogmas, and beliefs."

"Yes, in all honesty," replied Dr. Ade. "The more I think about what you said, the more I can remember. So, yes, thank you again." The apostle turned his head slightly, looked at him, and smiled in response.

"So, while you go have your tea, I will rush to the office and do my paperwork. I have one last question for today. I know I said this outside, but I can't be in your presence without having questions," Dr. Ade said with a grin. The apostle stood at the entrance to his room, turned to Dr. Ade, and replied, "But you already have all the answers you are looking for."

"I am very aware of this, but I still need your help with this last clarification for today," Dr. Ade demanded.

All right then. "What else am I here for if not to express life through nouns and verbs?" the apostle replied with a smile, his hand resting on the frame of the door that led to his room.

"Okay, my question is, how do you know all this stuff you're talking about?" asked Dr. Ade.

The apostle put down his hand, stared at him for a moment, and then gently broke his silence. "You have given me every word I have spoken. Search your heart for the answer you seek, for what you feel I know in me is already in you, as it is in all things. I'll see you tomorrow, Doc," he said as he turned and walked to his room.

"The night staff will come to you with your medication right after the handover; enjoy the rest of the evening," Dr. Ade replied, disappointedly.

MAKING GRIEF BRIEF

It was already past midnight, and in the silence of the psychiatric ward, the patients rested in their rooms, enveloped in the warm embrace of deep sleep and loud snores.

Few members of staff sat vigilantly at the doors of the patients who required close supervision, while the nurses on duty sat in the silence of the nurses' station.

There was a calm atmosphere in the ward. The lounge was empty, and the garden was peaceful. A serene stillness filled the air, with whispers from the staff echoing through the quiet halls. Breathing sounds could be heard from the closed doors of the patients' rooms. Suddenly, a loud bang shattered the silence, causing a rush of fear and anxiety to ripple through the ward.

The loud bang came from the room opposite the lounge entrance, where the new patient was staying. He often experienced emotional shifts, struggling with moments of deep distress. Thoughts of self-harm gnawed incessantly at his fragile psyche, as he would isolate himself for days without eating or interacting with his peers every time he had an episode. In isolation, the weight of his agony is palpable, a silent scream echoing through the emptiness of his mind.

On days when his emotional sky was blue, bright, and summery, the new patient stood in his room facing the wall and smiled incessantly without saying a word or speaking to anyone.

On days and in moments when his emotional summer sky turns dark and gloomy and the sun refuses to shine, he hides his smile and hits the wall and the door with rock-hard punches, smashes paintings hanging on the wall, and becomes agitated with the staff and other patients.

Young and full of potential, only in his early twenties, he often felt overwhelmed by his internal struggles. He had attempted to take his life in various ways, but each time was unsuccessful; he withdrew deeper into isolation, grappling with feelings of regret and emotional instability.

It was rumoured that he had experienced a significant loss in a fire, which led to a breakdown that strained his relationship with his family. The pain of losing his wife and children and all he had worked for intensified his sense of grief and depression.

Since then, he had struggled with feelings of hopelessness, trying to offer his soul to the hungry jaws of death. Yet, life always found a way to intervene.

That night, the hallway felt too dim, more like shadows than light. His room held a weight in the air, dense and unwavering, like grief before it names itself. He sat on the edge of the mattress, motionless, fingers curled into fists until his knuckles paled. Something inside him stirred–tight, breathless. His chest rose in short, urgent gasps, as though trying to cough up silence.

The corridor beyond his door creaked quietly. The member of staff nearby had mistakenly dozed off, lulled by routine and quiet. But quiet never lasted with him.

Then, without warning, he swiftly went for the door, pushed it open, and ran. Bare feet slapped the vinyl floor. The sharp echo sliced through the stillness like a siren. He was already in the common room before the first alarm was pulled. The two members of staff gave chase, but the boy reached the wall first. He banged his head once against the common room wall.

Then he did it again, harder than before. A third time followed—louder, heavier. Bone collided with paint, leaving a dull, sickening thud. Fingers clenched. Blood bloomed across the surface like a spreading bruise. A deep crack split the air, but the silence that followed screamed louder than the alarms ever could. A red loom spread across the wall, vivid and defiant, bleeding slowly, like something long held in.

Conversations halted mid-sentence. One patient wrapped his arms around his knees. Another stared, unblinking, slips parted in shock. Near the exit, a nurse's hand hovered over her alarm, fingers trembling. Further down the corridor, a chair scraped harshly against the linoleum as someone stood too fast.

Still, the staff moved, practiced, and gently.

A male nurse dropped his knees. Sliding a cushion beneath the boy's head. Another crouched beside him, palm extended, voice low and steady. "You're safe now," he said softly. "You are safe."

The boy's chest still heaved. His shoulders curled inward like armour, but the rage had drained from him. His eyes flickered—wild, wet, unsure. He didn't resist the arms that wrapped around him, didn't flinch as they laid him on the stretcher. Blood streaked his temple, a dark thread trailing back to the wall.

As they wheeled him out, the sirens remained silent. But inside him, his pulse still thundered. His gaze drifted upward, catching the flicker of the fluorescent light above. His face was pale, vacant.

Gradually, the ward returned to a sense of calm. Patients who had already settled into their rooms gathered in the lounge. Others sat outside in the garden, smoking or vaping. The earlier bang and the sound of alarms had kept everyone on edge.

The apostle stood at the entrance to his room, observing as the ward slowly regained its usual rhythm. He went down to the lounge to find out what had happened from the member of staff who had been helping the young man.

"O life, you cruel wretch! You punish us incessantly, unjustly, and without mercy. I've had enough of this young man's suffering, his desperate pleas for relief, and his futile suicide attempts to end his life! My heart bleeds with every shattered prayer he whispers into the mouth of death. How can life make him pick up the broken pieces of his soul after inflicting so much misery on him? "Life is unfair," the female member of staff lamented in her African accent, complaining to the male member of staff, who was trying to clean the bloodstain off the wall.

"I think so too," he replied in his Zimbabwean accent as he dipped the towel into the bowl he had with him. "The young man will have a big, permanent scar on his head if he survives this," he said.

"Absolutely, and it will give him even more reasons to spiral into crises. He'll probably feel more justified in thinking life has cheated him," she replied. Because now he would see it as even more rational to feel cheated by life," the female staff member replied.

"But then, who wouldn't feel that way? If life was fair to him, why cause him so much grief at such a young age?

Sometimes I wonder what our purpose is in this miserable shithole we call life. Why were we born if it seems like we are going to spend our whole lives in sorrow? If I were in his shoes, I would feel the same way, especially after life has turned everything he once saw as happiness into misery. Now, sorrow is all he knows," the male member of staff said.

I get even angrier when something happens and these pathetic sympathisers start saying 'God knows best.' I'd like to strangle anyone who says that to me. It's highly insensitive for God to deliberately inflict pain on the people he supposedly loves.

Are we like toys to him? Did he create us to entertain himself with our sufferings? If he is love, then he knows what it is like to love and how painful it is to lose what you love," the female member of staff again lamented, her eyes downcast as she spoke. She stood up and walked toward the door, bumping into the apostle, who stood there listening to her lament the whole time.

"Oops, you startled me, Apostle," said the woman, taking a deep breath with her right palm on her chest and her face pale.

"I am so sorry, my dear," the apostle replied calmly. "I didn't mean to scare you. Just take a deep breath, okay? You will be fine."

"Thank you, Apostle. I was just in my feelings, so I decided to go out for some fresh air. I did not realise you were standing there. It's been an eventful 35 minutes, and my emotions were all over the place. Seeing the guy try to hurt himself was so hard for me to take. Life hasn't been fair to him," she lamented again.

"Well, isn't that the purpose of life? she asked. To be born, to work hard to make a better life for yourself and others, to be loving to others, and then, just when it feels like you are winning, life rears its ugly head and stretches out its terrible hands, snatching everything you have laboured to build and inflicting pain in return. Isn't that the meaning of life, Apostle?" she asked. She lowered the corners of her lips and leaned forward slightly as she turned and sat down on the sofa from which she had arisen.

"May I sit next to you," the apostle asked gently. "Yes, sure, you may. The sofa is big enough," she replied, trying so hard to force a grin to sit on her pale-looking face.

"Thank you very much," said the apostle. "You are welcome," she replied. "I hope you do not mind if I ask you a question," the apostle inquired. "No, I do not mind. Ask what you want. If I can answer it, I will." she replied with a shrug.

"Why are you so angry with life?" asked the apostle.

"Seriously, you saw what happened a few minutes ago, didn't you?! Yes, people will call it mental illness, but is it fair? What's the point of living if all we do to be alive is grieve and lose?" she answered, her voice heavy with frustration.

"But everyone you love will die, and you will lose everything you own," the apostle replied.

It felt like electric currents were coursing through her body with each word she heard. She detested the term "loss," having suffered enough of it to make it her new normal. Her best friend had committed suicide after being raped on her way home from a work meeting. She had recently lost her boyfriend's father to cancer, and a few days later, a new employee had taken her place at work.

"Aren't people heartless, unfeeling, and inconsiderate?" She said it with a slightly raised tone, as pain could be felt in every letter that made up the words her heart poured out.

"Someone who gave everything to the company," she continued. "She was the hardest worker in the room. I know how dedicated my best friend was. She gave everything, every damn thing, and when life happened to her because of her loyalty to the company, they just moved on like nothing had happened."

"Judy would not have died," she said, standing up. "I thought life rewards those who give their all, but life was so unfair to her," she lamented with her fists clenched and her feet on the thin line between a scream and a burst of tears. "She was my best friend, Apostle," she lamented, sitting back down slowly and snorting her nose as she fought back tears.

"She was my best friend, and all she wanted was a good life for everyone around her," she mourned as she lowered her head and sat down to keep from sobbing.

Without saying anything, the apostle just stared at her. "Can I make you some tea or coffee?" She asked him to pretend to suppress the emotions she had just let out. "Thank you, but I am full," the apostle replied.

Although the truth hidden in the apostle's answer hurt her, her fear and worst nightmare were to lose and let go of what she loved.

"I respect your pain, my dear, but life shares grief with everything that lives," the apostle continued. Like trees in winter, leaves fall and branches break, but in this divine nakedness, when all that makes you majestic is taken from you, only then will you be reborn. Pain is the baptism for the spirit that is aware.

The spirit is born into a new light when the baptism is complete. The new light is full of understanding and freedom. The understanding that all of life is infinite allows us the freedom to realise that every loss is the birth of a new experience.

People strive ceaselessly to avoid the thought of losses because they are so convinced that they have made a profit by time trading. I've spent time building this, so I don't want to lose it. I have spent time building this amazing relationship, so I cannot afford to lose it. I have worked so hard for this job, so I cannot lose it. I have spent so much time and energy building this fan base, so I cannot trade it for anything.

What good traders we all are, trading pleasure for pain wrapped in a sheet of goals won and desires fulfilled. No wonder we have become so attached to the feeling of gain from trading time, treating it as if our lives depend on it.

But what can you possess, my dear? Are they just ideas that fall apart when compared to the most convincing fairy tales? Or are they illusions that promise false security? Do they speak of fulfilled desires, and goals achieved that lose their prestige in the face of a new longing? Or are they morals, values, and beliefs that crumble when faced with contradictory thoughts?

What can you possess? Can you possess figures as wealth, or figures as friends? Can you possess your self-image or your ego-projected reputation? How piggish, yet poignant, it is to know that you always want to have and possess everything you love.

You want to possess control because, in your superficial thinking, you can manipulate them in your favour to avert suffering. But you forget that the simple act of possessing is the root of all suffering. That's why letting go feels like dying.

The universal spirit, in its infinite mercy, seeks not to control but to guide and help you transform, so you may release the need to possess. Instead, you accuse life, God, the universal spirit, and your higher self of being unfair whenever a change occurs. And you pay for this course by losing some of the gains you've made and owned from the time you sold.

Nothing in nature possesses or owns except humans, not even the grave. It loses the body it holds to the terrible hands of termites and moths, and the insatiable hunger of the sand. To the grave, loss is life," said the apostle.

"But again, why should life give us these things if it does not want us to possess them or be attached to them? How can we truly love something if we do not possess or attach ourselves to it? For example, how can I be open to something if I am not attached to it? I think life should not let us experience these things if it cares so much about us not suffering. Instead, you're telling me that life wants to help me avoid suffering by giving me change, but the thought of being alive is suffering in itself," she replied as she passionately voiced her grievance.

"Life does this because it finds its meaning in death. What you refer to as gain or profit is the suffering and death of something else."

"Can I tell you a story," the apostle asked. "Yes, sure, I am listening carefully; the female staff member obliged."

I lived in my father's kingdom when I was just 7 years old. My father, the king, told me that I would rule the kingdom when I became an adult. As a child, I was served by housekeepers and servants. I wasn't even allowed to leave my room, which had everything I could dream of. The best Islamic scholars, great philosophers, mystics, and sages came from the city of 333 saints to teach me about the beauty of the stars, the charm of the moon, and the love of the sun. But I was not allowed to go to the garden, which was next to the back door of my room.

I was not allowed to experience the pain and suffering the world was experiencing because the prophets said I was divine and not allowed to see the outside world until I reached my teenage years.

I had everything I wanted. I kept everything I liked and never threw anything away, even when I grew tired of it.

When someone died, I was told they were going on a long journey. No matter how curious I became, I was convinced that the person would return soon. But time and distractions were my helpers. They helped me forget the things I lost, just like I kept my toys and other belongings, locking memories away with time.

One day, my father, the great king Mansa Musa, visited the city of the 333 saints with my mother, the queen. In the 15th and 16th centuries, the City of 333 Saints served as an intellectual and spiritual centre as well as a hub for the spread of Islam in Africa. Kings and queens, including my parents, visited the city for its festivals.

It was winter, and a small feast was taking place in the royal hall of the palace. I called it home. While the guards were distracted, I noticed the garden gate was open. I sneaked in through the back door, and to my astonishment, the first thing I saw was a tree.

I had never seen a tree before. I didn't know what it was called. It looked undernourished because its leaves were scattered on the ground.

To my astonishment, the closer I got to it, the more alive it became. I was both scared and excited, but my 7-year-old, curious mind led me forward, and I kept looking around, hoping the guards wouldn't catch me. If I were caught, it would mean the death of the guard on duty and a severe punishment for me.

The tree spoke with such eloquence and style that his words felt like ice in my ears and roses in my soul. It told me that its existence is not about its brown, plump trunk that people call a tree, but about the leaves that people experience and express their lives through.

It told me that for its leaves, childhood is its spring, youth is its summer, and old age is its winter. The tree loved its leaves so much, and it welcomed the birds that visited and made their home on it. But it learned not to own the birds, nor did it try to own the leaves that made up its essence, the beauty that drew the birds to it. The tree gave parts of itself to heal people and provide shade for the farmer. It shades the farmer when the sun comes out to play. When the sun went down, it gave its part to be burned as firewood for warmth during winter.

If it were attached to its leaves like humans are, people wouldn't have herbs to heal themselves or fruits and vegetables for their bellies. But humans reckon themselves as grander creatures, oblivious of the fact that their very existence is useless without the presence of the tree and its verdant leaves.

So, it appreciates the delights of loss because it understands that nothing in the cosmos is lost. But humans believe otherwise due to familiarity, an illusory feeling of ownership, and attachment. I feel sorry for them, the tree stated with its head lowered in sadness.

My 7-year-old self listened to what my freedom from myself would be. What my parents wanted to teach me through avoidance, a tree taught me in a few minutes through acceptance.

According to the tree, you humans suffer because you think you know everything. You think you are above life itself, but despite your superiority and supposed knowledge, you cannot accept change. True strength lies in our ability to accept and adapt to change, particularly in the face of loss.

Embracing these qualities is the deepest expression of wisdom and resilience. It is through acceptance that we find solace, and by being open to change, we can transform our grief into growth.

It sounded sad, but its face radiated a charming smile when it spoke again. Four of my leaves died this morning before you woke up, son. Some will die soon. But if they are lucky, the wind may ease their slow death by blowing them from my branch, which is their support, to the ground. There, they will give up the ghost and wait to be reborn in the spring.

Some of my leaves are still green, it said, even though their magnificence, which is evident in their green colour, may not last till midnight.

But what does a leaf have to lose? Dying is one of its superpowers. Before it dies, it enjoys its elegance for a moment.

For the first time, I felt something different. I never knew grief. I had always had everything I wanted, so I did not know loss. But today, the tree taught me the value of gain in loss.

Before I could blink, I saw a leaf fall from its branch. It fell with such pride and happiness, ready to be embraced by the icy winter ground. The tree knew it was time for change, and it celebrated the loss. Every lost leaf is a gateway for countless others to grow.

The problem, my dear, is not life; for you too are life. The problem is you're clinging to the things you are familiar with: your sense of ownership, your fear to accept change, and your inability to truly feel. You store grief inside you so much that it turns to resentment, which is the breeding ground for suffering.

Grief, like hunger, is just a feeling. You should accept it, feel it, so you have nothing left to store.

"My question to you before I return to my room is this: When loss knocks at your door, when change comes calling, when death visits wearing thick cloaks and serves you a cup of misery and a plate of sorrow, do you weep because what was served to you was bitter and hard to swallow? Or do you weep because you have lost what you thought you owned?" asked the apostle.

The female member of staff stood still, dumbfounded, her lips sealed and her tongue tied. The apostle stood up, wished the staff a good night, and went straight to his room.

The female member of staff, still speechless, had the feeling that the conversation was an epiphany. She stared at the male member of staff who had just finished cleaning up the blood stains on the wall and said, "I still do not understand why this man is here."

"Well, I guess for the same reason he just showed you," the male colleague replied sarcastically.

"See how you just listened to a delusional man talk about a tree speaking to him when he was seven. And here you are, saying that you cannot believe why the man is here.

He told you that his father is Mansa Musa, and you are still asking me silly questions. Can't you see that his symptoms have returned because he refused to take his medication as he should?

Thank God you have a plant in your house! Maybe you can talk to it like he told you, and it will teach you," the male colleague replied sneeringly as he threw the towel he had used to clean up the stain on the wall into the bowl and got up to leave the room.

"Well, I do not blame you," she replied. "You think he's talking nonsense? But you have always believed, as a Christian, that Moses spoke to a burning bush, and you're telling me you're not delusional either? Even the people who told you that..." She let out a long sigh, left the lounge, and walked towards the nurses' room.

DREAM CHASERS AND PURPOSE FINDERS

"Good morning, apostle; I hope you had a good night." I see you are sitting in this garden alone, enjoying the morning sun," Dr Ade inquired, inhaling deeply, shrugging his shoulders, and letting out a slow exhale. He walked over to where the apostle was sitting behind the flowers and remarked, "Hmm, it really smells like love and light out here."

"Good morning, doctor. It's good to see you again. I barely slept last night; sleep passed by my room and did not bother to stay with me. But it's a new day, and it will be back today, and then I'll be intimate with it," Apostle replied as the smile he shared with him forced itself out of his thick, bearded mouth.

"Will you sit with me and sip your coffee? You can also enjoy the love play I have been watching between the orange-coloured morning sun, the birds dancing and singing love tweets to the wind, and the wind tossing them back and forth."

"Sure, that would be great," Dr. Ade replied as he sat down in the chair next to the apostle. "Oh, nice view, I must admit. Wait a minute!" Dr. Ade exclaimed. "Are you telling me that the whole explanation you just gave is about the two black birds sitting on the roof?" he asked. His jaw dropped slightly, and his eyebrows rose.

"Yes, and you just missed the movie," the apostle replied, setting his coffee cup down on the table in front of him. "But the birds are chirping and flying around on the roof," Dr. Ade replied. "You missed the movie the moment you opened the door of your mind to let thoughts in. You did not see; you just looked. The birds had a purpose in life, but you only thought they were flying around. You are not wrong; you said what you saw," the apostle replied.

"Wow!" Dr. Ade exclaimed as though a cannonball had hit the walls of his ego. "Hmm, ok, let me digest that," he said, sipping his coffee a little and placing the cup back on the table.

"Since you know what it means for a bird to live for a purpose, you, as a human, should know what it means for humans to live a purposeful life," demanded Dr. Ade.

"When you say purpose, what do you mean?" the apostle asked him. "I mean, what are we here for as humans? What were we created for? What is the meaning and essence of life? That's what I mean when I say, What is the purpose of our lives?" And you know, you can be happy as a human being and live a fulfilled life if you know the meaning and purpose of your existence," said Dr. Ade.

"Are you not tired of inflicting suffering on yourself and constantly searching for the meaning of life and the reason why you are here? If you keep forgetting that breathing is the purpose, the meaning, and the reason you are here, you'll spend your life chasing shadows—like your forebears, who sought and found nothing, only to live on the lips of men and on the stones that mark their graves," the apostle replied. "Now you are swimming in the same whirlpool."

"Did I just hear you say breathing? Like, breathing is the meaning of life? Hmm, ok, very funny, but the answer was not really what I expected," Dr. Ade said. "Can you explain what you mean by breathing being the purpose of life?"

"Sophistication is to the human mind like a barrel of water in the desert, revered and beatified because conventional thinking has made it so. But when a thing sounds simple and easy, the mind sees it as sand, so common and disdained that the mind takes away all the value it carries while the feet trample on it."

So many things have man noticed on his way to Golgotha. If it looks noble, then it is worth carrying. He calls everything he lifts a cross, clings to it, and makes it his life's purpose—forgetting that his true purpose lies in the breath that keeps him moving toward Golgotha. Ask yourself thoroughly, Doc. Would there have been a cross if there had been no awareness of the journey? The breath gives the titles, the label, and its momentary value to everything you have chosen as your purpose in life today," the apostle said.

"How can that be?" Dr. Ade asked hastily.

"What good is it to be a doctor if the very breath that gives you life is gone?" the apostle asked in reply. "How could a tree bear fruit and flourish if no breath flows through its roots and trunks? How could a bird show its grace to the wind if it had no breath to help it flap its wings?

Your sages have taught you that being grounded means paying attention to your breath, feeling your aliveness, and being in the moment. Doesn't this tell you that just by breathing, you are fulfilling your purpose? Doesn't it open your soul to the reality that the presence of breath within you is the presence of God, of divine intelligence, and of the universe? Your awareness of that breath is the purpose of being.

Oh, how blind your thoughts appear and how closed your mind becomes when you think that your reason for living is buried in your conscious actions, fickle labels, and trophies. How did you learn to exhale and inhale? Who taught you to blink? It does not matter, does it? Yet, you call what you have learned through the teachings of other closed and deluded minds like yours a purpose. You think you are more valuable and knowledgeable than the birds and the trees. You believe that you alone fulfil the purpose of life, and they don't. You have given yourselves crosses to bear in the name of ambition and burdens to carry in the name of purpose, and still, you need more things to make you feel alive and give your life meaning and purpose," the apostle said.

"Do you mean to say that I should not have aspirations and that I should not pursue dreams?" Dr Ade interjected with a question as he stared at the apostle with narrowed eyes like an eagle searching for precision. But in his case, he was trying to make sense of what he had just heard.

"So, what's the point of being alive?" he continued. I'd feel worthless if I woke up without a dream to pursue or a goal to realise. Okay, so to make sense of this, you said earlier that we love each other, right? Are you saying that love is no longer a purpose in life? If love is the purpose of life, as you stated last time, doesn't that contradict what you just said, and that breathing is the main purpose of life?" Dr. Ade inquired, looking confused.

"What if you were taught to chase your dreams just to keep you asleep? The dreams you chase are the only things you feel give meaning and value to your life. But, when life changes, when everything you've attached yourself to is taken away, you feel sorrow and depression. Without those things, existence becomes worthless, for there is no longer any reason to live," the apostle replied.

"Humans are so quick to forget that they are the creators of their misfortune. They take on sorrow and suffering in many forms, like ambition and desires, and then ask the universe to lighten their burden.

The water knows that its purpose is to flow. Whatever it does while flowing, is but a cross it bears on its journey of purposeful living. It can flow into a bottle of wine or a hole and form a pond. Being in a pond or a bottle is not its main purpose. Flowing is the purpose of its existence. Everything that flows through or into it is just a tool to make its flow exciting and eventful.

The endless thought of needing something to live for pulls you away from happiness and peace. It automatically sets you on a never-ending search for purpose, for something to attach to, and the persistent longing for something to live for instead of just living, breathing, flowing, and being.

When you check the pulse of a dead person to see if they're still alive, what do you look for except the presence of breath? If the presence of breath is the ultimate sign of life, doesn't that mean that breathing is its only purpose? And before all things, you call purpose, there is simply this–an act, an experience, a moment that makes your breathing feel playful, eventful, fun, and valuable?

The simple act of breathing, which manifests itself in everything that carries this life force, is all that is worth living for. It is the greatest form of self-love because, when you breathe, you give God a chance to express and experience itself. Breathing is also the greatest act of vulnerability because, when you hold your breath, you hold the flow of life.

The importance of your goals, dreams, and aspirations hinges on the truth that they are powerful tools for life to express and experience itself. For this reason, they should be done with care, with love as the lubricant and breath as the engine. So, know that breath itself is enough. Life does not need a purpose to be meaningful, because anything the soul attaches to rather than connects to, we automatically limit our experience of it.

If music is only what you appreciate and live for, you will never have a chance to accept, understand, or experience existence on the days when it looks like a movie. The trees know this truth better. They submit to life because they understand that a reason to live is an illusory sense of duty.

Simply being its authentic self is all it has to live for. This awareness allows it to bear fruit when the time comes, without pressure and stress. It becomes so vulnerable to the wind in winter; it sheds everything that gave it its splendour and charm during summer because its sense of vitality does not depend on something that cannot be without breath.

Breath is life's force, and life's force is energy. It is what animates living beings. It is the divine power that gives all living things their vitality and strength. Energy is everything. So, an energy that needs something to feel alive, meaningful, be, is like an energy that needs itself to be itself.

I tell you again, as I told your ancestors, you need nothing to live for. You are already alive, and breathing is the purpose of life. When breathing is made the only purpose, everything is done. Breathing is experienced as valuable and good in every moment of existence because it is done with purpose."

TIME TRADERS & ATTENTION SEEKERS

"I've heard enough, old man. Just shut up," the young man snapped, his voice sharp and booming like a crack of thunder. His eyes burned with a wild fire, unblinking. "So that's why you locked me in that cage... just so you could come here and sell out the very people who needed you?"

An American-born Congolese in his mid-twenties, he stood tall, shoulders broad and tense, bare chest rising and falling with every ragged breath. Ink curled over his dark skin—each tattoo telling stories of battles, seen and unseen. A red scarf hung around his neck, fluttering slightly in the breeze like a flag of rebellion.

The member of staff at the garden gate flicked a lighter, shielding the flame from the wind, helping him spark the cigarette wedged between his fingers. The small flame danced briefly before he took a long, angry drag.

“But... they weren’t talking to you. How did you even hear what they were saying from here?” the member of staff asked, frowning.

He exhaled a thick cloud of smoke right into their face. “Fuck off,” he muttered, voice low and venomous. Without waiting for a reply, he turned and strutted toward the table where Dr. Ade and the apostle sat, his steps heavy, deliberate. Two members of staff flanked him like shadows, never too close, never too far.

“Looks like you’re out here giving this sellout some life advice, old man,” he sneered, stopping a few feet away. “But don’t waste your breath. He ain’t listening. He’s one of them. Tried to break me but couldn’t. So he threw me into the seclusion room like a dog.”

His finger jabbed toward Dr. Ade, eyes narrowing.

“I saw your lips move,” he spat. “You think I’m not watching? I may not care for books or small talk, but I can read faces like street signs. That’s survival. That’s what keeps you alive in the jungle. I see the snitch in you, even under that Viking beard of yours.”

His hand shook as he pulled on the cigarette again. “Don’t fuck with me.”

The apostle raised his hands slightly, voice calm, steady. “Son, this isn’t about you.”

“Yeah,” Dr. Ade chimed in gently. “Take a breath. You’re alright. Sit down, man. We’re just talking—nothing heavy.”

The young man let out a harsh laugh and flicked the half-burnt cigarette to the ground. It landed with a hiss on the damp grass. He crushed it beneath his heel like a dying flame.

“Talking?” he barked. “You’re out here babbling about ‘purpose’ while we’re trapped in a war. A fucking mental war.”

His voice cracked, but he kept going, louder, sharper.

“You want the truth?” he asked, pacing. “I said I didn’t want to work. That’s all. That’s my crime. And now I’m locked up in a padded room like I’m some monster. This place isn’t for healing—it’s for control. They don’t want a Black man to be free, not unless he’s broken.”

Dr. Ade and the apostle sat quietly, the silence between them thick as smoke.

“They send these fake-ass motivational speakers into the hood, preaching lies paid for by people in suits. Telling you to dream while they bleed you dry. But I ain’t no fool. I live by my own code.”

He moved closer to Dr. Ade now, who slowly stood.

“Back up, please,” the doctor said calmly.

The young man obeyed—barely—stepping back with a smirk as if daring him to flinch. "All I want is to chill with my fat black queen, roll a J, and watch this fucked-up world burn. I ain't working for no man. 'JOB' means just enough money to survive—and I'm done surviving."

He pointed at the apostle now, eyes twitching with fury. "You better stay woke, old man. That Judas beside you? He's a traitor—sold out the community, then had me thrown into this damn madhouse. He's one of them—with the Feds."

His teeth clenched so hard; his jaw pulsed. Dr. Ade remained motionless, eyes locked onto his, not with fear—but with something deeper. Pity? Understanding? It only made the young man angrier.

"He ain't saying nothing because he knows I'm right," he snarled. Then he reached out and slapped the staff member's shoulder with a mocking grin. "He wants me to work for him. Me? A gangster? Shit! I'm not built for that. I'm built for war."

He ripped open a packet of tobacco from under his arm and rolled another cigarette with practiced speed, eyes never leaving the apostle. His fingers trembled slightly, betraying the storm still raging inside.

"You need to breathe, son," the apostle said softly, voice like the rustle of leaves.

"I Am Not Your Son." The words hit like gunshots. "And don't ever tell me to calm down again."

He stared between the two men, breathing heavily, rage coiled tight inside him like a spring ready to snap.

"You're on his side now?" he barked. "You think I don't see through you too?"

Suddenly, he hurled the lit cigarette across the table. It landed inches from the apostle's chest, burning out in a puff of ash. He lunged forward, fury written all over him, but the member of staff stepped in just in time, blocking his path like a brick wall.

"Back up, please," Dr. Ade repeated, firmer now.

He didn't speak. He just spat. The thick glob hit Dr. Ade's shirt, sliding down slowly like a silent insult. Then, with a shove to the staff member's shoulder, he turned and stormed off.

The metal trash can by the garden gate clattered to the ground behind him as he kicked it over, the sound ringing out through the quiet air like a final scream.

Two members of staff followed, their pace quick but cautious, trailing the weight of a storm they couldn't stop—only contain.

"What a boy!" Dr. Ade exclaimed, wiping the spittle from his shirt with a white cloth he took from his pocket as he returned to his seat. "When was he admitted? I have not seen him since I have been here. Why is he here? He seemed so livid with you; what did you do to him?" the apostle asked.

"Well, he was in seclusion. He was really in a bad state when he came in, with a diagnosis of drug-induced psychosis, and it looks like it's his first episode. He also has a history of ergophobia, which is why he kept talking about working and not working. He believes that Tupac is his father," Dr. Ade said.

"Oh. I see, now it makes sense," the apostle said, nodding his head slowly in agreement.

"He hit a member of staff on admission four days ago, so he was sent straight to the seclusion room to prevent further incidents and exacerbation on the ward. His parents told me that he hates to work; it makes him so nervous that he dabbled into drug use and abuse, but he will be fine," said Dr. Ade with a grin on his face.

"I cannot blame him. You know, when I think about it, we all have a bit of ergophobia in us. Let's face it, Mondays have a way of terrifying us all," he said, Dr. Ade, bursting with laughter.

"Is that why I saw you talking to yourself as if you were one of us?" the apostle asked sarcastically. "You mean the other Monday?" said Dr. Ade as they both laughed out loud.

"Now you are taking a piss at me again, Apostle. I was just in my zone, you know," Dr. Ade said with a smile.

"But do you think it is normal to automatically become anxious as soon as it is Monday, even if you have no job, but as soon as it is Friday, you feel a kind of inner relief?" asked the apostle.

"Well, to be honest, in all the years I have been a psychiatrist, I have never really thought about it. It could be some kind of mental conditioning the system puts on every adult, I guess," he replied with a subtle grin on his face.

"Why are people always in a hurry?" asked the apostle. "What do you mean by "always in a hurry'? Can you elaborate?" asked Dr. Ade with a slightly puzzled look. "The young man clearly said that you only live once; what does that mean?" asked the apostle.

"Don't we only have one life to live?" Dr. Ade asked the apostle in reply, with a shrug.

"We all do, and this idea gives us a sense of purpose and duty. It's the same thing I was saying earlier, when we were talking about purpose and all that before the boy steered the conversation off track. Honestly, the boy was stating facts to a certain extent, even if the rest of the claims he made sounded grandiose, to say the least," Dr. Ade said with a laugh.

"And at the same time, it is a powerful tool for shaping and conditioning the ego mind," replied the apostle.

"What do you mean? Can you please explain that in more detail?" asked Dr. Ade.

"You are always in haste because you only live once, aren't you?" asked the apostle.

"Yes, and?" Dr. Ade prompted him.

"And that is what constitutes the core of that statement. Because you are rooted in the idea that you only live once, you become an avid trader of time in the marketplace of existence. And what is time management, if not the ability to be a skilled trader of time? Time is formless, and the only viable currency that exists in form.

To give it meaning, we must formalise it, allowing the mind to fully engage. Its formalisation created the idea of binding time to existence itself, and these binding impacts everything within it. Life, as we experience it now, is bound by time. So, trading it becomes inseparable from the act of living itself," the apostle replied.

"Are you saying that living depends on how efficiently we can trade time? Dr. Ade asked, slightly confused.

"Why do you work, doctor?" asked the apostle in response to the question. I work to earn a living, replied Dr. Ade.

"Are you dying?" asked the apostle.

"Well, I might if I do not work," Dr. Ade responded wittily. "Does that mean I am dead?" The apostle asked again.

"I still do not understand what you are getting at, Apostle," said the doctor.

The apostle paused for a second and then continued. "All I am saying is that I am not working, and neither are the other lads here, yet we're still alive. If that's the case, then the reason for your haste is not because you only live once, but because you are afraid you will only die once. The ultimate fear of death is born from attempting to cage life in the ticking hands of time.

Work, by its divine essence, is life's canvas where the mind becomes the tool through which we create, express and experience. Work is not what sets the mind in motion; it is what keeps it alive. Pathetically, the act and art of work, made to be a medium for self-expression and life experience, have been creatively transformed into a platform for time trading.

Traders have made it the most proficient platform to trade time with, adding a sense of fulfilment that comes with it. This sense of fulfilment sparks a feeling of aliveness, and because the mind, by its nature, connects most with tangible things.

Physical currency is thus created as an exchange for attention, helping to make time, which is intangible, something we can exchange. When you are not making progress or gaining valuable experiences because you're not focusing on meaningful opportunities, a sense of emptiness can settle in. It gradually saps your energy, leaving you feeling disconnected and lost.

Verily, and I say to you again, we are all time traders, for to live in this plane of existence governed by time is to trade it. Some people trade it for a week's or a month's wages; others for ideas gained from words read and spoken. A few trade it for assurances and affirmations, others for compassion. Some trade their time for affection and laughter, while others sell it for chains and trauma. Some trade their time for a place in heaven; others sell it for thoughts packaged as products.

Some sell theirs for trophies and medals that they get from judging those who sell theirs for wages, salaries, words, emotions, ideas, and chains; they are amazingly renowned judges. Their trophies and medals make them feel fulfilled, they feel alive, and that makes everyone even."

"What then is time?" Dr. Ade asked. "What is it, if not moments commercialised with price tags tied around its neck," the Apostle answered.

"This I say to you today, as I said to your fathers: The wise man is he whose source and meaning of existence are rooted outside of time. Moments, to such a man, are precious, divine, and worth more than gold. Such a soul is aware that life has given us the opportunities to act, express ourselves, and amass life experiences. Such a soul is a diligent trader, for its mind instantly serves the purpose for which it was created.

He understands his role as a trader of time, consciously trading for the right experiences and attention, so he can express himself. His sense of aliveness and self-realisation is not bound by anything in time," the apostle said, standing up, adjusting his belt, and sitting down again.

"That is remarkably profound, Apostle. I'm not sure how your mind arrives at such a thought, but when you are through, you'll have to reveal who you truly are," Dr. Ade said, gazing at the apostle with a sly smirk on his face. "It's saddening how we judge. I once scolded a younger cousin of mine for not trying to work, not unaware that he was always in his room writing. It was not until he published his first article that I discovered what he had been quietly creating. Everything you said makes sense to me, but one thing remains confusing. Could you explain what you mean by the 'proper attention' a man needs to express himself?" he asked as his brow furrowed in confusion.

"Deep in every circle is a line; in the heart of the cradle is a grave. Deep in the consciousness is the mind, and buried in the heart of the time trader is an attention-seeker," replied the apostle. "Attention is the lubricant for the mind that supports its smooth running and effective time-trading.

In vain will the trader trade if attention is absent at the moment of trade. The presence of attention is the prerequisite for a trade well done and experience well gained.

How precious is your attention? Sadly, you trade it for hollow experiences, as barren as a winter tree. How can a brand sell what you don't need yet make you crave it, if your attention isn't fully engaged? Your attention shows up, sharp in suit and tie, always ready to broker the deal between your mind and the lure of your attention seeker," the apostle said.

"Words are magnetic forces; they attract attention. Words that are shaped into stories attract attention. Stories presented as problems hold attention. Products created to solve problems in stories grab your attention by convincing your mind to want something you don't need.

The attention seeker starts by turning a product into a story –a tale of a problem and its solution. This story is crafted to capture the time trader's attention. What we used to call advertising is simply a way to highlight the problem and fix it. Once the story hooks the trader, publicity steps in, convincing them that this problem is theirs to solve. Wrapped in the illusion of scarcity, desire, and the sparkle of FOMO and trends, the problem now feels urgent and personal.

The tool you call marketing is just a way to communicate the attention seeker's stories to the time trader's mind, selling the solution wrapped in a product. Marketing strategies are creative, subtle methods that improve communication between the attention seeker and the time trader, making it more effective.

The time trader, with a mind now shaped by desire, wraps himself in the cloak of want and decorates his conditioned mind, wears the cloak of want, and adorns himself with the jewellery of FOMO and trends. Like waves crashing on a rock, the pull of need and desire keeps his mind restless, never at peace until it's satisfied. Satisfying the need is the cure for the problem, so the time trader trades his attention and opens all the gates that lead to his mind for the attention seeker to plant his product. The trader buys the story packaged as a product that carries the cure for the problem, and his needs are met until another story is brokered between his mind and the attention seeker.

I ask you today: how much time can you trade and how much attention can you seek? Is love the torch that helps you in your search, or does your ego light your way as you seek? Is your attention guarded by thick walls of understanding, or is it so free that anyone can take a piece of it? Are you trading with the highest bidder, or are you seeking attention due to a lack?" the apostle asked.

"This is so overwhelming that I cannot even find the right words to create answers," said Dr. Ade, wiping his face with his bare palm and inhaling deeply and exhaling slowly.

"Why are you here?" Dr. Ade asked.

"When will the event you spoke of last time begin?" asked the apostle, pretending not to have heard Dr. Ade's question.

"That does not sound like an answer to the question posed, sir. But I am not going to persuade you anyway," said Dr. Ade, sounding discouraged because his question was not answered.

"For the mini-event, the occupational therapist has switched up the idea, and in terms of the process, everything will be more interesting, engaging, and conversational. The idea will now take the form of a focus group. The aim is to promote cooperation and community among the patients on the ward. The old patients can get to know the new ones, and as you are the oldest here by age, it would be nice if you could share your experiences with us," replied Dr. Ade, looking very enthusiastic. "I think everyone should hear and also have a share of the pearls you have served me.

"That is indeed a good idea, and it will be a pleasure for me to share everything I can remember," said the apostle. "By the way, I am expecting a delivery by the end of the week." "Do not worry, I have got you. But wait a minute; you do not have a phone, so how did you place an online order? And you said you have no one here, no family, and no friends?" Dr. Ade asked, looking confused.

"Isn't everyone here my family? Aren't you my friend?" asked the apostle Dr. Ade.

“But you know what I mean,” replied Dr. Ade, standing up and taking his now-empty teacup from the table.

“I will be on my way to the nurse’s station now, Apostle. The time I spent here was a really good trade,” Dr. Ade said with a smile, “and I am grateful, even if you did not answer some of my questions.

“All is well, Doc. The answer you seek you already have, and I thank you for your attention. I have sought it, and you have given it to me. There is no greater love,” replied the apostle, with a radiant beam on his face. “I will leave immediately to take a quick shower and get ready for the event,” he said, walking slowly behind Dr. Ade as they both entered the building.

THE GODLINESS IN CREATIVITY

The hall hummed with quiet excitement. Rows of plastic chairs stretched across the room, many already filled by residents—some leaning in to whisper, others shifting anxiously in their wheelchairs. A woman with soft grey curls clutched a mirror to her chest like a secret. Another adjusted her vibrant headwrap and smiled at nothing in particular. Their faces were expectant, touched by something warm and unspoken.

Sunlight poured through the wide windows, scattering gold across the tiled floor like spilled grace. It bathed the room in a soft, holy glow—almost as if the sun itself had slipped in to bear witness. On the stage, fabric banners fluttered gently, announcing: You Matter: Mental Health Awareness Week.

The colours—bright pinks, soft blues, gentle yellows—seemed to breathe life into the room, like hope had been hung on the walls.

Movement pulsed through the space—staff weaving between patients, laughing quietly, handing out slices of cake and berry smoothies. Two doctors, fully dressed in their scrubs, leaned against the back wall, hands wrapped around cups of hot chocolate. Near the front, eight women from the female ward sat tall, their dresses colourful, eyes curious.

Nine male patients huddled just beside them, nudging one another, cracking jokes between sips of fruit parfait. The only empty chair belonged to the apostle—a quiet vacancy in the corner that felt somehow sacred.

And yet, the atmosphere sparkled. There was laughter—low, steady, blooming across glowing faces. The air was rich with the scent of melted cheese, cocoa, and something cinnamon-sweet. At the back, a long table sagged under the weight of spring rolls, cupcakes, deep-pan pizzas, and vivid bottles of soda. It felt like a holiday that had tiptoed into the middle of the year.

Then the karaoke began. One by one, patients braved the mic—voices shaky at first, then louder, freer. Some waved their hands like pop stars; others dissolved into giggles mid-song.

Those too shy to sing simply pointed to random numbers and received surprise tracks—rap, R&B, highlife, gospel. No judgement. Just joy.

Then came the shift. The beat dropped—Afrobeats blared through the speakers. Laughter erupted as a nurse challenged Dr Ade to a dance battle. He flung off his white coat like a cape, twisting and grinding with playful abandon. But the nurse outshone him—hips loose, arms fluid—and the room roared with cheers. Even Dr Ade bowed low in mock defeat.

"Britain's Got Talent better watch out," he gasped, breathless and grinning.

A male member of staff turned the volume down. The occupational therapist stepped forward, hands clasped, a soft smile curving her lips.

"Hello everyone," she said gently. Her gaze swept across the room, eyes lingering on every face. "Today was meant to be my birthday celebration. But I thought—why not make it more than that? A chance to come together—patients, staff, old and new. So we can keep healing... as a family."

Then, without warning, the atmosphere shifted again.

The apostle entered.

He moved with quiet gravity, wrapped in a flowing black kimono that brushed his knees—timeless, dignified. Heads turned. Conversations stopped. A nurse near the door whispered, "He's here."

The OT's eyes lit up. "And there he is," she beamed, her voice bright with joy.

Applause broke out, rising like a wave.

He said nothing. Just placed a hand on his chest in quiet acknowledgment. His presence grounded the room. He was the oldest patient—and yet, somehow, the soul of them all.

"What have I missed?" asked the apostle. "You did not miss much, just that you did not get to see us sing or see the nurse beat Dr. Ade in an Afrobeats dance challenge," replied one of the newly admitted patients, triggering a burst of laughter in the room.

"She did not beat me at dancing. I just let her win; you know I am a gentleman," Dr. Ade replied hastily, trying to save his face from the shame of having lost the dance battle.

"Listen up, everyone," the OT began to speak again. "As I was trying to say before our long-awaited speaker for today arrived," she said, staring at the apostle. "We have done things differently today, so it will be an interactive session in conjunction with the refreshments, and the apostle will be leading this, am I right, Apostle?" she asked him.

The apostle smiled in unison and in complete agreement with what she said, but his thick grey beard hid it so that his eyes had to take over where his hidden lips left off, even though he didn't say a word.

"We will take that as a...yes, so I want us all to welcome our apostle, but first, you, like everyone else, must choose a song."

"How am I supposed to do that?" asked the apostle. "Ok, it's like this. We have the numbers three, seven, eleven, and twenty-two to choose from, and then the DJ will play the song. You can also dance to it if you feel like it," said the OT with a big smile on her face, while the others waited anxiously to see which song the apostle would choose.

"That sounds amazing," the apostle replied, and after a long pause, during which it seemed as if he was imagining the songs to the numbers in his head, he slowly raised his head and requested the number seven.

Everyone was excited to see what the song would bring, but silence swept through the room like sandstorms in North Africa.

The member of staff playing the DJ turned up the volume as the piano melody introduced the blessed sound of John Lennon's voice.

"I am not surprised," yelled Dr. Ade from his seat, whereupon a roar of laughter rang through the room.

"Imagine" is a song for days with a cool sound. Yo, you are a weird old man with a vintage taste in music, the American-born Congolese patient sitting a few feet away from him hollered.

"I know, the apostle loves good music too," replied the OT.

"If only today's musicians were as thoughtful as John Lennon, if only they sang their songs from the core of their being and not from the intoxication of drugs and all that, then maybe we could love playing and dancing to the music of today as we did in the 70s and 80s," said the British-Pakistani patient in her mid-30s, who carries a mirror with her everywhere she goes and stares at it impulsively.

But how can she say that, a nurse whispered to Dr. Ade? She sounds like she was born in the 70s, when she's only thirty-three. You know she struggles with identity crises, so you shouldn't be surprised by what you have heard, Dr. Ade replied in a muffled voice.

"Niggers ain't creative any more. Everybody is ganging. The system is shit, so they promote shift craft," the American-born Congolese patient yelled again in disgust.

"Well, it looks like we have something to talk about," the OT said aloud. "Thank you, Apostle, for choosing such a great song. As I was saying before the apostle picked his number, this will be an interactive session. The apostle will share stories from ancient Africa, where he's supposedly from, right, Apostle?" She asked, flashing a dazzling smile, elbows bent, fingers interlocked, and her gaze fixed on the apostle.

"Isn't that the reason for this moment?" the apostle asked her calmly. "Of course, it is," she replied hastily.

"So, anyone who wants to ask something can tell us their name and the reason they're here with us, so we can all get acquainted."

"Yo, Moses," the American-born Congolese patient shouted from his seat, just as the nurse dropped her last word for the audience to hear. "Talk to me about creativity because these niggers out here are just creating trash in the name of art."

"Did I just hear him call the apostle Moses? These 'Oyibo brought ups' have no respect, sha," the Nigerian member of staff said in a low tone, glancing at Dr. Ade, who just smiled and did not say a word.

"No, my love, you do not just ask randomly. The pattern is to tell us your name and why you are here, so we can get to know you," the OT said in reply to the young man's question to the apostle.

"Why are you comparing?" The apostle asked, standing up and walking towards the seat that had been placed in the middle of the room where the OT once sat while she moderated the event. "There is no need to compare, for none is creative." At this point, everyone turns their attention to the light pouring out of the apostle's mouth.

"What makes you think you are creative?" He asked, staring at the silent audience. "Is it because you create harmonious sounds and call it music? Or, is it because you build houses that are higher than the ones your fathers built in Babel? Well, birds do that too.

The nightingale sings so well that the whole of nature falls at its feet when it hears its voice. The bald eagle builds its nest so turgid, refined, and highly aesthetic that the wind testifies to its splendour when it whistles."

“So, what makes you creative?” The apostle asked, pointing to the American-born Congolese. “You cannot compare me to animals, man. Animals do not have consciousness. That alone makes me creative, so what are you saying, man?”

A closed mind is indeed as blunt as a child’s toy sword; how, then, can it cut? If a chisel is edgeless and unyielding, how can it sculpt a masterpiece?

If the mind is shackled by rigidity and ego, how can the divine spark within ever soar free? Only when the soul breaks its chains can the creator truly create.

The architect erects a building and calls himself creative, but fails to see that sand and stone were already creative enough to stick together, vulnerable enough to be shaped, and transform into a house.

He praises himself without realising that he has done nothing. Just as the energy deep within everything brought the idea of the building to life, the same energy within him brought it into being.

The same story is told of the farmer in ancient Kemet, who calls himself an exquisite farmer. He boasts of having planted the best plants, forgetting that creativity was the energy that connected the soil, the seed, the sun, the wind, and the rain—the same energy that made him put the seed in the ground.

But he praises himself alone without acknowledging the other elements.”

The artist blew his trumpet so loudly and expressed his praise clearly in words.

"Like Picasso, I Am.

My mind is majestically imaginative.

It sees God in the devil.

It sees water in fire and bubbles in heat waves.

It sees sight in blindness and perceives Mary in whoreness.

It counts the thousand words on the lips of the dumb.

And a thousand walks in the limbs of disabled people.

It sees nuns as nymphos and priests in fraudsters.

It sees angels in witches and nightmares in wishes.

It sees lines in circles and snow in the rain,

And the pleasures adorably planted in pain.

So, like Picasso, I am.

Like God, I create.

My hands are so Midas.

Whatever it touches turns to gold.

Give it five and watch it increase tenfold.

It creates youth when it touches the old.

Give it the forest and watch these hands create a road.

It creates laughter with the recipe of sadness,

Genius out of every madness.

From nothing, it creates anything.

My hands have a touch of divineness.

Serve its ideas dead as Lazarus,

and watch it give them breath like Jesus.

So, like God, I create."

"So, what distinguishes you from these creators who sing their praises? Are you not all farmers? Are you not all architects? Are you not all artists who constantly sing empty songs of praise to the creations they carved with blunt knives? What can a blunt knife cut?

What can a chisel that shares a blank strike carve? How can a brush with frayed bristles paint? How can an ego-ridden mind that holds God in chains express and experience itself?

That which should be creativity in its divinity has become self-destruction in the hands of your ego-driven self. For the ego expressing and experiencing itself is akin to a soul in its conditioned state.

For such a soul, its creative zone has become its purgatory.

It always keeps things to itself,

Creating things just to stack them on their shelf.

It manifests the same things it feels scary to imagine,

Sitting in the dock and still being the judge—

Sentencing itself without parole, shredding its life into pieces,

while praying to be whole.

It lives every day in fear

as though its beat is on death row.

Its crime is imaginatively creating

laws, the same laws with which it repeatedly judges and compares its creations.

It watches itself drown, thinking it is swimming.

Always imagining love yet creating pain.

It calls itself a Samaritan, yet it does good for the praise.

Always seeking freedom through its art,

Yet adorning its mind with chains.

Always keeping to itself, yet in every creator's lane.

Always touching others and turning them into gold,

Yet touching itself with the same hands, but covered in thick gloves.

It brags about being God, a farmer, and an architect with a touch of Picasso.

It always thinks it is creative, but boxing God eventually.

So, like the man powered by his ego,

that which you call creativity is merely self-destruction.

The Congolese, like everyone else in the room, were speechless; no one spoke a word. Silence entered the room and held everyone's lips, listening to the apostle and watching dumbfoundedly as he continued to speak.

"Man's creativity is as boundless as his divine self is free. When God is freed from its shackles, boundaries and limitations, titles and labels, it expresses and experiences itself in all its glory, splendour and greatness. However, when God is freed, its shadow–the ego, remains shackled behind the thick bars of love, vulnerability, acceptance, and chains of self-belief and diligence.

The product of this expression and experience of the divine energy within is what you call creativity. The divine energy in man connects it with its replica in everything present in nature. This connection is God expressing Himself through man as a vessel, like other vessels outside of man. How vain for a sword to claim creativity, when the true artistry lies in the hand that wields it.

Verily, I say to you today, as I said to your fathers, the truly creative man is the man whose soul is without form and void, such that the divine energy floats freely above the waters within him. The freedom of God in such a soul is shown clearly in the light that the soul radiates through the things it creates.

A soul like this is referred to as creative because it is susceptible to the universe's embrace and is willing to express itself through it, letting it choose its shape and fill its voids.

Remember today that the things that hold your ego bound in every moment of creation become tools that allow the spirit to be as naked as it can be so that life can pass through it.

Love will shed the cloak of judgment that your ego mind once wore; the cords of comparison will be torn by total acceptance. The spectacle of difference will be stripped from the eyes of your mind, and your heart will shed the leaves of attachment. It will become as barren as oak trees in winter, and in that barrenness, life can possess it until it becomes fruitful through its self-expression, and the fruit of self-expression is what your father called creativity.

When you create, do not forget to take heed lest you fall, because there is one thing your fathers never told you about creativity: its eternal relationship with the ego. The more your creativity evolves, the more your ego evolves. Creativity also needs the help of the mind, and the mind is the citadel of the ego.

To be safe is to nourish the soul, for the more love enlightens the soul; the more the soul is overwhelmed as it becomes saturated with love. And in this saturation, creativity is born and it flourishes effortlessly, with love taking the lead and the ego losing its grip on the mind.

Thus, the body is inspired to create while being driven and guided by love, in love, and through love.

THE PARITY IN BEING

The room remained relatively quiet as he spoke his last words. The young man stared at him in awe. The dark-skinned nurse from Ghana standing behind the man noticed how stunned he was by his look. It was obvious he had just heard God speak through a schizophrenic old man he used to make fun of.

"My name is Abena, I am from Ghana. I am a mental health nurse, as you all know," the nurse said, her voice breaking the silence. She smiled elegantly, revealing her dark-coloured gums and bright white teeth, as everyone in the room cheered.

"Thank you, nurse," the apostle replied gently, rotating his chair to face her squarely as she spoke.

"For me, the essence of existence is that we recognise "the God energy' within us, just as you said, Apostle. I believe that if we allow this divine energy to express itself in us, then that is truly living. Maintaining a balanced and spiritual lifestyle can often feel like an uphill battle.

Practices like meditation, eating a clean diet, and committing to a vegan or vegetarian lifestyle are not only time-consuming but can also be financially demanding. Between the rising costs of healthy food and the mental effort required to stay focused, it can feel exhausting to maintain that equilibrium. Finding true balance amidst these pressures often seems more difficult than it's made out to be. But if your spiritual awareness is a priority, I think it's worth the sacrifice," she said with a shrug, "or am I wrong?" She asked over the background noise of the other employees grumbling as she spoke.

Why is life unbalanced? Why must one thing suffer so that the other can exist? Should it be so, or is balance in life unattainable? A female patient diagnosed with bipolar disorder, sitting ten metres away from the apostle, asked him, interrupting the Ghanaian nurse.

There was total silence once more, with everyone's ears waiting to hear what he had to say and every heart longing to receive the jewels he would spill.

Alas, he turned his head slightly, stared at the lady, and spoke. "Is life unbalanced, or have your eyes taken on the role of weighing scales as its life's mission? What is the urge to find balance in life? It is the result of the intimacy of judgement and comparison. What have your eyes not compared, and what has your heart not condemned in judgment?

Eternally clinging to extremes and always reproaching life for being fickle and unbalanced–how unfairly have you treated it! Life serves you variety, yet your scales perceive differences. Like a pendulum, you swing momentarily, but like stamps on a letter, you get stuck at one extreme, and from this extreme, life is perceived and judged.

Look within, examine all that you do, and see. Do you see it as it is, or do you perceive it according to the value system of your weighing scales? Your gullible mind has so often perceived heaven in extremes, just as it has blindly worshipped the allure of comparison.

Why do you compare? Why do you judge? Is it not written in your holy books, as it is engraved in your heart, that the universal intelligence has made all that it created in absolute splendour and perfection?

Is universal intelligence not the breath in your lungs? Is it not life itself? Are you not life itself, expressing and experiencing through human costume?

Aye, I say to you; as I told your fathers, shine the light of consciousness upon every heart that clings to the body bearing the tongue that sings of life's imbalance. For in the heart of such a body, you will find a conscience afflicted with the disease of self-comparison and self-condemnation.

Verily, I say to you that even the very thought of creating or seeking balance in life is an act of weighing life on your ego-enriched scales of judgment and comparison. For an ego-driven life, reality is always unbalanced because the ego's attachment to extremes is the source of its being. For a life shaped by love, where balance comes naturally, extremes are just illusions—like prisons made to look like castles.

The balance to which I speak to you today, as I did to your prophets, is rooted in moderation. In this moderation, love finds its source, and within this source, the essence of life's balance is found.

No one spoke a word; only eyes stared at the apostle, mouths open, hands folded, and attention focused on his presence as if a prophet were speaking. The apostle paused, eyes closed and lips sealed in complete silence, as if downloading the next gem to drop. He opened his eyes and continued speaking.

"The ultras are prisoners of their demise, limiting life's experiences and expression while stuck in oubliettes painted with the dazzling colours of ideas, decorated with accoutrements crafted from beliefs, culture, and illusory schools of thought.

From the windows of their dungeons, which they have called palaces, they compare and judge everything else. In their eyes, the others who cling to the other extreme are wrong and live wrongly, and those who dwell in the middle are lukewarm. They cannot choose because they do not cling to any extreme.

They cannot decide because they are not stuck at either extreme. How exalted they are in judgment; how good they are at comparing! They weigh everything. They are inwardly unbalanced, and outwardly they sing with the loudest tone and the highest voice about the imbalance and unfairness of life.

The man who feeds only on greens feels that the man who feeds on what the moment gives, regardless of what his system requires, is irresponsible. Meanwhile, the latter perceives the former as ignorant and does not want to enjoy the bounty of life.

The man who fights rebelliously against conformity thinks the man who happily conforms is a lover of his chains, forgetting that rebellion is a refined form of conformity. Additionally, the man who has discovered the charm hidden in the illusory freedom of conformity finds the rebellious man to be a nuisance.

They have both made the extremes their permanent abodes. For them, they are alive, but all they do is judge and compare. Life is lived and perceived through their scale, so why won't they tirelessly seek balance?

But can balance in life be found at the extremes or in the middle?

Why not study nature, my beloved, if you truly seek to find parity in being?

Does the tree see life as imbalanced by clothing it with colourful and genteel leaves in spring, only to leave it unclad to be frayed and broken by the harsh embrace of the December winds?

Does the moon perceive existence as asymmetrical when people praise the sun for its light during the day and see its light as less valuable because of its intimacy with the night sky?

Does the grass perceive life as crooked because it has always been trampled by the same elephant it is trying to feed and sustain?

Adopt the ways of nature, my beloved. Nature acts in moderation, and in its divine balance, it is centred in the core of being. So, to be righteous is to be present, responding to life's flow, doing what is needed, when it is needed, and at the right level. By simply being, the God within is centred, and the life without is balanced.

THE SATORI ON LIFE AND DEATH

The man sat hunched in the corner, swallowed by the shadows where the light from the window couldn't reach. A strip of white bandage was wrapped around his head like a quiet warning.

He didn't move much—just stared at the floor, eyes glazed, fingers twitching now and then as if holding onto thoughts he couldn't name.

Across from him, the apostle sat still, hands resting loosely on his knees, watching without staring. The silence between them was thick, pulsing with things unsaid.

Then came the voice—barely a sound.

“Does balance mean both life... and dying?”

The man didn’t look up. His words drifted out like smoke, fragile and slow. The apostle didn’t answer. He just listened, his body leaning forward the way one leans toward a candle struggling not to go out.

The man’s lip twitched. His shoulders rose, then sank like waves with no shore. “I don’t think there’s balance in any of it,” he said, his tone low, scraped from somewhere deep. “We wake up. We try.

We laugh sometimes. We hope. But then it all falls apart—dreams, people, the parts of us we don’t show.” he paused, swallowing hard.

His right hand clenched into a fist against his thigh.

“And still,” he continued, quieter now, “I’d choose death. Every time.”

The apostle didn’t flinch, though something in his eyes darkened—just slightly.

The man shifted, fingers digging into the fabric of his trousers. “In death, nothing hurts. There’s no tight chest, no spinning thoughts, no waking up wishing you hadn’t.” His voice cracked, but he didn’t stop. “I imagine it’s quiet and soft like floating in water with your ears under, and everything above j ust disappears.”

He leaned his head back against the wall. The bandage brushed the plaster. A faint wince passed across his face.

"I wait for it. Every day. But it never comes. It's like death is... scared of me. Like, even death doesn't want me."

For a moment, the only sound was the distant hum of fluorescent lights and a bird calling far outside the window. The apostle's hands slowly folded together, his breath steady, grounded.

But the man kept his eyes on the floor, as if afraid that looking up might make his pain too real.

Or worse—make it seen.

"Who taught you that the opposite of life is death? How absurd is it for the mind to regard death as an end? Did your life begin with birth? What makes your mind regard death as its end?" The apostle asked him.

"I do not know anything about that," he replied. "Are you saying that death is not the end of life?" he asked the apostle. "That would be a bizarre thought," he said, his voice tinged with sardonic laughter.

With a smile on his face, the apostle stared at him and said, "Is that why you want to stop the melodious sound of your heartbeat so badly? You have been persuaded to believe that death is the end of all sufferings. But if life ends with death, as you have been led to believe, why do dead things transform after they decay?

You might have been taught to say that it is mere science, but were you not also taught that only living things change?

You plunge into the grip of death, seeking refuge from life, all the while forgetting that death's true opposite is not life, but birth. Life, in its boundless and eternal essence, has no opposite. It is an endless continuum, unbroken and infinite. Birth and death are the only episodes, the fleeting scenes in the divine film of existence. Life is energy itself–indestructible and unyielding, incapable of creation or annihilation; it is only transformed, continually changing from one form to another.

For the soul drowning in the stream of ego-consciousness, death seems to be the end of life, but even death is still the birth of life into a new earth, one that is formless. It is the door that leads back to the space from which conception is formed," he said, staring at the man. Then he turned around, looked at the audience, and spoke thus.

"What have your souls been taught about death? The suicidal soul sees it as an alternative to escape the pain of life. The religious soul lives in denial of death, praying daily to ward it off, forgetting that the denial of death is a denial of life. A soul, afraid of thieves, shuts its doors - yet it locks out friends and loved ones as well."

You all pray for a quiet life, but are blind to the truth that death is the surest gate to reaching it. But is a smooth-sailing life worth living? Can a boat row on still waters? Why do you fear what is inevitable?

Who told you that eternal life is without death when death is the essence of life? Are you so fixated on how you want to live that you do not think about how you want to die, as if death is not part of life?

You have been made to fear death so much, like a bird learning to flinch before the storm; no wonder life itself has become such a weary flight." I ask you again, my beloved, why do you fear death? Is it the shadow of your ego that whispers to your soul, convincing you that you'll lose something you never truly had? The life you toil for is not even your own. How can you lose something you do not even own?

To experience the divine bliss of death, I tell you again and again, my beloved, is to study the tree in winter. Stripped of all it once wore, it stands naked against the biting wind, knowing it has nothing to lose, for it never grasped a single thing in the first place. What the human mind perceives as the death of its leaves is only a harbinger of a new birth in spring. It is not an end, but a quiet promise that the soil of loss will give birth to something new.

What we mourn as endings are the unseen seeds of transformation, waiting to bloom with the warmth of spring. In every death, there is rebirth, and in every ending, a new beginning. So, it is for a man. You die momentarily, and in each new moment, you are born again. Death, on the other hand, my beloved, is the foundation upon which all memories are built.

It is not worse than birth, nor is birth better than death. Both are but portals, through which we pass to touch the eternal rhythm of life, experiencing its bondless flow, manifesting in temporary, yet vivid, forms."

"You speak of death like you are not afraid of it," the man replied after the apostle had spoken.

The apostle stared at him and spoke again, with everyone's attention focused on him. "Why do you fear what is destined for you? Do the green leaves of the sycamore tree tremble in terror when autumn calls? Do they drown in fearful thoughts of winter, afraid of losing their green hue as they turn gold, yet quietly knowing that death is not the end, the beginning of something new?

Hence, it shines and lives purposefully in summer because it will embrace winter when it comes, in love and perfect fulfilment.

Aye, to accept death and its promise is to be liberated from the fear of it, for every death is a gentle reminder to other souls to truly live. Unfortunately, you have let your ego crash into the driver's seat of your mind, taking control with relentless force, its presence spreading like a poison, inching deeper into the heart of your soul.

Embracing death as an escape from life, instead of embracing it for what it is, strips it of its essence.

If only a soul could truly grasp its profound connection to others, realising that the death of one bleeds into all who are bound to it, it would no longer seek to escape life's crushing burden. Instead, it would face death with a ferocious choice, to endure the agony that births true purpose in the chaos of existence.

How excruciating to realise that the grave where your ego-shattered soul is cast is both an irreversible end and a dark womb, where life is reborn into a new realm, with death serving as its relentless mediator.

Why then do you act as if you fear death, yet you are so afraid of life?" The apostle turned and asked the suicidal patient.

Still stunned by the life-changing words of a schizophrenic old man, he nevertheless continued to speak. "I do not think I am afraid of life. I, uh, I just do not know; I cannot even organise my thoughts properly. You have lifted a burden from us that we all carry with great fear and dread, but if death is all you said it was, then what is life?" The man asked the apostle in reply.

"Life is what remains when the restlessness and disquietude of death are overcome. You think and tell yourself that you are afraid of death, but what you fear is life itself," replied the apostle.

"But how can that be?" Dr. Ade asked from where he was standing, near the entrance to the event hall.

"Just as you have been taught by those who flaunt their ego and call it wisdom and wear titles like cloaks...," the apostle replied.

Dr. Ade shrugged his shoulders and remained silent as the apostle continued to speak.

"I still wonder how one can fear life. It makes no sense to me. I hope he did not hear what I said." Dr. Ade spoke in a very low tone, or maybe he did. This old man can be strange, whispered the member of staff standing next to him. "I am sure he didn't hear it. The female Nurse seated beside Dr Ade replied with a plastic smile. I barely heard what you said," as she turned her head to focus fully on the apostle.

"If you are not afraid of life, why are you thinking of suicide?" said the apostle, staring at the man without blinking. "If you are not afraid of life, why do you wage wars to end it, make rules to govern it, pray, cast it, and bind it? If you are indeed not afraid of life, as you claim, then why do you try to control it? You are only trying to control what you fear.

You do not simply fear death itself; you fear the very essence of life that it will strip from you. The true enemy in the depths of your ego-driven mind is not death itself, but the fierce, irretrievable life it will tear away from your grasp.

What have you not done to life? You abridge it in others, you abridge it in yourself, and you blame it for your choices as your fathers did in their days in Eden.

You compare it, judge it, get angry at it, own it, govern it, condition it, criticise it, nullify it, condemn it, and make a puzzle out of it. What has life done that you treat it with great contempt and disdain?

You persistently ask about the meaning of life, but you never ask what life is not. You forget that knowing what life is not opens the way to knowing what life is.

Breathe in, breathe out—that's what life is all about.

That which cannot be seen, that which cannot be touched, but only felt and experienced.

How utterly senseless it is to ask another to unveil the meaning of something they cannot even fathom. To ask someone to enlighten you about the unseen, the unknowable, is to mock the very essence of understanding itself.

How annoying and mortifying it is to ask someone else to tell you something that only you can experience! You have done the same with the idea of God as you have done with the idea of love, and sadly, with the idea of yourselves. All these concepts are the same: love, God, life, and the idea of you.

Aye, all that my tongue can share and all that my lips can let go of are words that express the essence of what life means to me, which is how much of it I have experienced and how much of it I have expressed. So, you have to define life yourself and give it your personal and exclusive meaning. Consumed by your irresponsibility, you've desperately sought others' voices to define your existence, allowing yours to wither. In the end, you loathe your truth, for it feels empty and raw, lacking the elegant metaphors, the crafted verbs, and the polished nouns that others seem to wield effortlessly.

How do you think a crow would define life? Imagine an ant defining her life or giving meaning to it based on the descriptions and definitions given to her by the bird. It would see life as unfair and cruel. The bird flies, but the ant does not. It would also be wrong for a fish to define its life and give it meaning based on the definition that the sheep gives it.

You carry out all of this with the depth of your entire knowledge and awareness. You forget that your feeble mind acts and reacts based on the definitions of life that you give it.

Just as no two things are the same, it is also meaningless for two different things to have the same meaning and the same definition of life. Instead of your ego-damaged mind accepting this fact and rejoicing in the bliss hidden in diversity, it fights, argues, compares, and dogmatises what should be relative, and in its relativity, its expression becomes whole.

Verily, I say unto you, as I said unto your fathers: Just as the duration of life, like love, is transitory, so is its meaning.

The meaning of life is forged in the moment it unfolds. Thus, determined by the moment in which it is expressed. For the tree, winter is the silence of detachment, spring is the fiery rebirth, and summer is the exuberance of youth. The same is true for water. It shifts its essence–what it is in a cup is not what it becomes in a pot. Life, like nature, wears many faces, each born of the moment.

But if the water, like the tree, were human–its meaning of life shifting with every breath, you'd call it madness; its words would be nothing but a repulsive contradiction. Yet here you are, sprinting towards the very death you claim to despise as if it were the only truth that could silence the chaos of life.

Irony, it seems, is the only thing you chase with any certainty. What does it truly mean to live if you run from the very thing that gives it meaning?

FROM SOMETHING TO NOTHING

At the far end of the room, in a threadbare armchair near the window, she perched like royalty on a forgotten throne.

Her compact mirror lay open in her hand, a silent companion. The small round glass glinted each time she shifted. Her fingers moved with practised grace: lashes brushed, lips lined, foundation smoothed into caramel skin like a second mask. Her eyes never left her reflection.

She whispered to herself, lips moving as if mouthing a prayer only she could understand. Her expression flickered—first dreamy, then sharp, then distant again. Then her voice rose, cutting through the quiet like glass.

"What's the point of breathing if no one sees you?" she said, words sharp but musical. "Might as well be dead, innit?"

Her laugh followed, sudden and wild. It melted into a smile too wide to be calm.

"I mean, how can you love what you can't see?" Her gaze never left the mirror. "But me? I'm visible. Always. I'm a queen, yeah?"

She tilted her head, admiring her glow under the flicker of overhead lights. Her dark curls, full and untamed, cascaded down her shoulders like storm clouds about to break. She adjusted her top with care, letting the fabric fall just right—just enough. Her hips swayed as she crossed one leg over the other, a silent performance to a captive room.The apostle sat nearby, watching her without interruption. His mouth parted to speak, but she waved him off with a flick of her wrist, eyes still fixed on herself.

"I'm the hottest in this palace," she declared, arching her back, stroking her collarbone, then running her hand down her side. "They should crown me, not her. The other queen. What's her name again?"

She giggled, leaning forward just enough for the room to lean in with her.

Her gaze swept across the silent staff and patients, their eyes drawn to her like moths to flame. she grinned, pleased.

"I can't die, darling," she whispered, almost sweetly. "Queens don't do that. We rule." She turned towards the apostle, lips parted in a pout. "Tell me, Mr Apostle... how do I make the world mine?"

The apostle stared at her intensely but never said a word. Feeling disappointed, she took out her mirror, stared at it for a few minutes, and started wailing loudly. Everyone was shocked as her mood changed due to the silence of the apostle.

"No one pays any attention to me; everyone else has had their questions answered, but I am the only one who is ignored. If I were already queen, you wouldn't be ignoring me," she complained, tears slipping down her cheeks as she wiped them with the hem of her brightly coloured dress, revealing a glimpse of her caramel-toned thigh. The members of staff beside her quickly stepped in, knowing all too well what was coming next–another one of her dramatic outbursts that everyone had come to expect.

The apostle's gaze lingered on her, quiet and unreadable. He said nothing. Not a word. His silence stretched thin between them like a thread ready to snap.

Her face faltered.

She blinked. Once. Twice.

Then, slowly, she reached into her lap and pulled out the compact mirror again. Her fingers trembled slightly as she flipped it open. For a moment, she stared into her reflection—eyes wide, lips tight—searching for something only she could see.

Then came the sound—a sudden, piercing wail that split the room in two.

Heads turned. Conversations hushed. The atmosphere, once uneasy, tipped into something heavier. The young woman's cries tumbled out, raw and jagged, echoing off the tiled walls like sirens.

"No one sees me!" she shouted, her voice cracked and trembling. "Everyone else gets answers. But me? I'm invisible. You'd never ignore me if I wore a crown!"

Tears streamed down her cheeks, carving thin, shiny lines through her carefully painted face. She rubbed them away with the hem of her dress, lifting the bright fabric just enough to reveal a flash of bare thigh—whether by accident or design, no one could tell.

Two members of staff moved quickly, quietly—one crouching beside her, the other placing a gentle hand on her shoulder. Their faces were calm, practised. They knew this script by heart.

And just as fast as the storm had come, it passed.

Her sobs softened into giggles. Her posture straightened. A glow lit up her face, like the sun breaking through clouds.

"I am a queen," she whispered with a breathy laugh. "Thank you, thank you all," she added, giving a tiny mock-curtsy without standing, the mirror still tight in her grasp. She turned her head to the side and covered her mouth with one hand, her shoulders bouncing with laughter as if she were being adored by a crowd only she could see.

Then she sat down with unusual care, crossing her ankles, tucking her dress just so. Her eyes drifted back to the mirror, her reflection drawing her in like a magnet. She laughed again, softer this time, to no one in particular.

Silence took hold of the room once more.

It wasn't the quiet of peace—it was the thick, stifling kind, heavy with discomfort and breathless. Chairs creaked as a few shifted uncomfortably. Eyes avoided one another. Something in the air had changed, like the drop before thunder.

And in the centre of it all, she giggled—alone in her spotlight, the only sound in a room full of watchers.

"Speak to us about how we can become better versions of ourselves. When we do, we not only dress better, but we also feel better, act with purpose, and make wiser decisions in life," the occupational therapist who hosted the mini-event asked the apostle. "I think that's what Miss Rosa was going to ask when she said she needed tips on how to be queen," she said with a smile, gently rubbing her palms together.

"Aren't you weary of becoming so many things other than yourself? You are always striving. But who are you? From the very moment you took your first breath on this stage we call existence, you've been chasing a phantom of yourself. When will you stop the endless pursuit of becoming and simply be?

When will you stop speaking and learn to truly see?

Did your prophets not share my words with you that true being is stillness? For in stillness, the greatness of God's expression and experience unfolds. Being is the purest form of its essence, untouched by the turmoil of becoming.

You crave perpetual evolution, drawn to an electrifying adrenaline rush that fuels your ego, offering you a brief yet intense sense of power and hollow achievement.

Yes, how fiercely you indulge your ego while relentlessly transforming, how ravenous your hunger for recognition, and how fragile the very foundation of your self-worth is. No wonder you're never truly satisfied. The apostle declared this, locking his eyes with the audience.

What greater version of itself could an eagle ever long to become in its desperate quest for acceptance, admiration, and love? What more magnificent incarnation could the sun ever be, rightfully called the sun, to blaze with brilliance, and to be revered and adored?

Woe to such love! For if love, acceptance, and value are only offered on the condition of becoming a specific version of oneself, they can only persist as long as that version holds value, leading to an endless cycle of self-reinvention and constant drive to evolve.

The palm tree knows that it doesn't need to strive to be a better version of itself to become a palm tree. It understands that all it must do is embrace what it already is, unwavering in its authenticity. In radical acceptance of its nature and its vulnerability to change, it stands rooted in the flow of life, evolving naturally without losing its essence, without becoming, but simply being, like a raging river carving its path, never losing its true form.

What have you not become to be accepted, celebrated, noticed, loved, and admired?

Does the star have to twinkle at noon for it to be relevant or worthy of acceptance? No, it merely is. Yet, you push yourself tirelessly to become a better version of yourself–sacrificing your values, your truth, your essence–suffering but smiling anyway, all for the approval of others.

Who told you that you are not as magnificent as you are at this moment? Who convinced you that a better version of yourself is more worthy than who you are in your divine state? Who sold you this belief? Who conditioned you? What mirror do you stare at yourself with, and what reflection do you hold up as yourself that you loathe, compare yourself to, and judge yourself with?

Aye, how attached you are to the reflections of what you are supposed to become instead of being fully aware of who you are.

You've turned the idea of self-love into a toxic drive to constantly judge and improve yourself, chasing after a "better version" that will never satisfy. This is Barmecidal love. This kind of love promises growth but leaves you empty, always wanting more. In this cycle, you forget that these versions are transient and ever-changing. The truth is, your divine essence is eternal and unchangeable. Instead of chasing after an ever-shifting version of yourself, the message here is to recognise that you are already whole and worthy, just as you are.

But for a conventional sense of acceptance and a conceited sense of self-realisation, one chooses thought over substance and ends up losing oneself.

So, how can you be a better version of yourself if you haven't even found and accepted yourself yet?

Who are you? Are you deluded by the reflection in the mirror, clinging to it like a purse under your arm, unwilling to let go of the illusion it creates of who you think you are?

This mirror is warped by societal standards, ratings, labels, titles, pronouns, and verbs, reinforced by culture, the opinions of others, passing trends, and the ego-driven mind desperate for validation. As the proverb goes, 'A man is but a product of his thoughts; what he thinks, he becomes.' You've allowed this illusion to define you, clinging to a false sense of self that is nothing but a fragile construct.

You value this illusory reflection highly and work tirelessly to maintain it and convince yourself that you are becoming a better version of yourself.

Why have you chosen not to learn from nature, my beloved?

The apostle asked, staring at the audience, turning his head slowly from left to right and from right to left while he kept speaking.

"Water, in all its splendour, is still water, even if it is poured into the most expensive glasses. It flows from the deepest oceans or stagnates in ponds. It doesn't need to be a better version of itself to be water. For it knows that it cannot be more or less of what it is in its purest essence, and any attempt to be more is to lose what it already is. To become is to cease to be, and to be is simply being.

Verily, I say to you again, as I mentioned to your prophets in times past. In comparison, reality is veiled, and shadows are perceived as substance. The constant comparison between who you are and who you think you should be, believing it to be self-love and the pursuit of becoming a better version of yourself, is nothing more than an illusion your mind creates.

Haven't you been told that a version is only an imitation of the original?

Yet you call it self-love, dropping your original self to be something you think is better. When all there is to do is drop the foggy ideas that cloud your mind and the illusory reflections you have adopted as yourself that keep you from being your original self in all its ultimate divinity and nothingness.

To be original means to be nothing. To be nothing is to be godly. By being nothing, one wears the skin of righteousness. Nothingness is space, and in this space, everything can manifest itself, depending on the energy prevailing at the moment. From nothingness you have emerged, and by being nothing, you become everything.

Everything was formed by one source: the divine energy and supreme intelligence that you call God. Everything that Midas touched transformed into something valuable, as it was created out of nothing. Therefore, the realisation that you are nothing in the moment opens your consciousness, like daisies in the sunlight, to the awareness that you are everything in that moment," said the apostle.

"But how can I be respected in this data-driven world we live in, where everything is categorised, labelled and evaluated? To be respected, you have to do something relevant. One of the things that matters and that I think you should value highly is your reputation. But what kind of reputation can you have if you are nothing?" asked the Viking-looking maintenance worker, who was listening attentively to the apostle and leaning against the wall next to him with his arms folded.

"And you know what they say—that a good name is better than riches, silver, and gold," he added.

"The idea that a good name is better than riches has bound people to words, labels, titles, nouns, and verbs. What is the meaning of a name if it is only a fruit of thought, whose lifespan is so impermanent that it fades with time? What value does gold have if its value is wrapped in ropes of conventional thinking?

Aye, sands and stones have proved more valuable than gold. Have you ever seen a well-built house, whose foundation is not made of concrete, adorned with gold? Isn't concrete moulded into a paste from a mixture of sand and stones? Yet, you call it nothing—ordinary and banal, because you step on it, spit on it, and pee on it.

But gold you revere, calling it precious stones, and would die for it, just as you would for names, titles, and labels. Why spend your life guarding what death will inevitably steal, when your breath fades and your soul departs?

What value is a reputation to the dead if it becomes nothing more than an epitaph? That which you call reputation, bestowed by a man who does not even know himself, you guard with all your strength and might.

Repent from thy myopic thinking, my beloved, for there is no reputation in a name but that which gives the name value, and breath in its verb form.

Therefore, my beloved brethren, breath is God and God is nothing and yet everything just as breath is. To be nothing is to be like breath, like water, vulnerable, constantly evolving to be what you are in complete accordance with the moment. When your sense of reputation springs from this awareness, you become conscious of being all that you are and also conscious of being present while being nothing.

BAG CHASERS AND MONEY DOUBLERS

"Hi lovelies, if you need anything, you can ask the staff and they will attend to you. There are also crisps, crumpets, Jaffa cakes, Lancashire Eccles cakes, hot chocolate and scones," and "our Nigerian sister has prepared extra Nigerian jollof if anyone is interested," The OT who hosted the event said to the seated audience seconds after the apostle finished his last speech, with a grin on her face.

"Can we at least get some cigarettes or a lighter, or is that not part of the menu?" shouted the 22-year-old Nigerian-born, British-raised university student, who had been admitted to the ward eight days ago with a diagnosis of Oppositional Defiant Disorder (ODD) and Attention Deficit Disorder (ADD).

“Ask nicely, son; there’s someone in the garden who can help you with that,” Dr. Ade answered him as he walked to meet the apostle where he sat.

As Dr. Ade approached the apostle, appearing as though he had a lot of questions stuffed in the breast pocket of his neatly ironed striped shirt, the six-foot man from Zimbabwe, in his mid-sixties, who had not spoken to anyone since his admission, finally spoke, to everyone’s surprise.

For more than 14 days, he has been withdrawn and isolated from others, constantly talking to himself, sometimes about different currencies, or talking angrily to himself and complaining about his money in the bank, about things he has to buy, or about money someone owes him.

In moments when he is not complaining, he laughs at himself, boasting about his wealth. Rumour has it that he was once an accountant at a big firm. Some said he was a tax consultant, but others claim he suffers from money dysmorphia, manic depression, and obsessive-compulsive personality disorder.

“After you, then,” said Dr. Ade, looking at the patient and recognising from the way he discreetly raised his hand that he probably had something to say.

“Cheers,” he replied calmly and smiled at Dr. Ade. Something he had not done since he had come here, which seemed and sounded very strange to the doctor.

The apostle stared at them as the man from Zimbabwe turned to him and asked, "How much is enough money? Is the love of money the root of all evil, as I have been taught all my life? Does it make all hearts evil because they strive for, want, and desire more money? Talk to me about money, because it seems I cannot live without it."

Dr. Ade then made his way to the empty seat next to where the apostle sat while the man spoke. "This is no coincidence," he said to himself. How did this man know that the question he just asked was the same one I was about to ask? He asked himself as he turned the chair around and sat down to listen to the conversation.

The man from Zimbabwe, on the other hand, sat upright and concentrated on the apostle. This time, he was not talking to himself or calculating numbers on the piece of paper he always carried with him, like a soldier with a rifle, but he listened attentively to the apostle as he began to speak.

"It is beguiling how much wealth man has made, as though it were the noblest synonym for 'breath.' But how much breath does one need for the lungs to declare their surrender? How much food must one consume before hunger is extinguished forever? Since money has become the lifeblood of your egocentric soul, its absence leaves you gasping in a void, as if life itself has drained away, leaving you a lifeless shell.

Yes, in your insatiable wants, the love of money is rooted. In your wants, too, your ego finds eternal refuge. Haven't you been taught by your prophets and sages of old that the ego gives life to abysmal intentions?

What is reflected on the pages of your mind when your eye perceives money and your heart beats for its lack or abundance? Your culture calls it the bag, and to fail in its pursuit is to condemn yourself to a life of struggle, poverty, and unfulfilled potential existence that is barely worth living.

Great thinkers have often said that money is the answer to all things. Yet, even King Solomon, with all his wealth, and Mansa Musa, with all his unmatched riches and grandeur, could not buy more breath when death came calling. In the end, all their treasures were of no use in the trade fair called life, where existence itself is the only true currency. And so, they learned the striking truth: in amassing everything, they found the one thing wealth could never secure- control over their final moments.

If it could answer all things, just as your hungry hearts were starved to believe, doesn't that make money the second name of God? Have you not been told by your priests and teachers that God answers all things?

How much have you been conditioned to spend your life chasing ideas that are passed off as currencies, yet constantly complaining about a life full of stress and strife?

In the days of your ancestors, cowries were the currency. The same currency for which your ancestors killed, fought, died, and lived has now degenerated into a fashion accessory.

Over time, cowries became obsolete, and as the human system evolved, new standards took hold. A new form of legal tender emerged, swiftly adopted and solidified, shaped by society's shared understanding and influence.

Your fathers stopped chasing cowries. They started chasing coins and banknotes made of brass-plated steel, paper, and other materials from the earth, replacing the tiny mollusc shells that also came from the earth.

So, how can you be poor? Didn't your ancestors teach you that the earth is yours? Why then do you pray, cast, bind, kill, fight, and hunger earnestly for what is made from the earth that is already yours? Why do you choose to suffer for lack of knowledge when everything can be manifested through work and total belief in yourselves?

Yes, the system is in upheaval. The new money is now made of numbers and cryptos, the raw materials grown from the system.

So why do you think you can stop chasing numbers when numbers are the backbone of the system, and virtual reality is an illusion?

You have crucified life and time, shackling them to your whims, forcing them to carry the weight of grief and burning wrath with every passing moment.

You curse the days that give you no riches, calling them terrible as though they owe you something. And when wealth graces your hands, you bow to the day, as if it's your victory. But in this frantic chase, have you truly seen what's lost, in the silence of the hours that slip away?

How you despise being loved for what you give, yet you do the same to life and time, chasing money and forgetting their value. You forget that you are life, living a short human experience. So why wouldn't money control your joy or plan?

Fear the love of money, for it is the blackened earth where evil grows. Each dollar you crave, each piece of paper you idolise, feeds a monstrous tree of corruption, tightening its grip on your soul. If you give in to this hunger, the tree will rise, shadowing every part of you and poisoning your heart. But if you have the strength to burn away the desire, to destroy the root of greed, the tree will fall. Its grip will loosen, and you'll remain free from its dark influence.

Yet you pray, cast, bind, fight, kill, and suffer for the absence of money, when no room has been made for it to dwell in. When it passes by your presence, you repel it with hatred and disdain, poisoning the heart that should have embraced it.

Your ego-driven mind is constantly flooded with ideas that stimulate its fixed attachment and endless pursuit of money. Being alive therefore, means being constantly on the hunt. Happiness, well-being, attitude to life and vitality therefore, depend on how much you can chase, grab,, and take with you.

Verily, what you love loves you, and what you hate hates you. That which you give room to remains, and that which you water grows.

So, how did love produce evil, my beloved? Can an apple root produce orange fruit? Can an eagle lay quail eggs? Does evil need love to exist? Or, is love a synonym for evil in the heart of your ego-driven soul?

Every root that springs from the soil of love will burst forth with love as its unshakable fruit, while every heart poisoned by evil will bear the rotting fruit of its wicked seed–its darkness consuming everything in its path.

Free your heart from ego, for wherever it holds sway, suffering follows in its wake. But when love commands your every step, it creates joyful rhythms and harmonious melody.

Truly, as I told your fathers, it is the fear of the lack of money that nourishes and waters the root of all evil. Yet, astonishingly, when you perceive money for what it truly is–a mere tool to express and experience love, the love for it becomes the very seed of all that is good.

"This is so profound," Dr. Ade said to himself as the man from Zimbabwe stood up and moved towards the apostle.

"Thank you for that wonderful explanation! Now, this place feels like home," the man said to the apostle.

"Everywhere is home, and you must make it so," replied the apostle.

"I'll go outside for a quick smoke and then come back for the rest of the conversation," the man from Zimbabwe said again. "Do you want a cigarette?" he asked the apostle.

"I do," replied the apostle with a smile on his face, and he slowly rose from his chair. You should have those thick beards trimmed so that your smile shows better," the man from Zimbabwe suggested to the apostle as they both laughed and walked out of the hall, down the corridor, and towards the garden.

Some of the patients and staff walked ahead of them while the rest were still sitting in the hall. Some of them went to the dining area to get something to eat.

The event feels... therapeutic," Dr. Ade said as he walked beside the occupational therapist. Their steps were slow and measured, following the apostle and the Zimbabwean man through the wide glass doors that led to the garden.

The OT gave a small nod, brushing a strand of hair behind her ear. "Hard to believe the money man finally opened up—right before his transfer," she said, her voice laced with quiet wonder.

Dr. Ade glanced at her. "Money man?"

She smiled and shrugged, hands deep in her gown pockets. "It's what everyone calls him. He's always muttering about cheques, coins, and foreign accounts—like his mouth only knows the language of currency."

Dr. Ade let out a low laugh, shaking his head. "Funny thing is, he asked the apostle the exact question I had in mind. I held back because I could feel he needed to speak first. The timing... too perfect to ignore."

The occupational therapist raised a brow, as though weighing something invisible in her mind. “Maybe all your psych degrees paid off—reading minds now?”

“No,” Dr. Ade said, his tone dropping to something more serious. “You did this. Your patience, your creativity — I just watched them unfold.”

The fresh scent of earth and lavender drifted into the air as they stepped into the garden. A few patients wandered around or sat on benches, soaking in the late afternoon sun. Somewhere in the distance, birds rustled between trees.

“I still don’t get it,” the OT muttered. “An older African man with a pile of diagnoses—schizophrenia, dissociative identity disorder... and yet when he speaks, it feels like scripture. But people dismiss him as delusional just because he says things that aren’t... common.”

Dr. Ade squinted toward the corner of the garden, watching the apostle settle on a wooden bench under a wide-leafed tree. “It’s not just what he says,” he replied quietly. “It’s how it feels when he speaks like something ancient comes alive in the room. I can’t lie—there are moments when I sit with him, and I wonder who the patient is.”

The OT let out a breath she hadn’t realised she was holding. “Maybe that’s the point. Maybe we’re not supposed to have all the answers. All I know is... he wasn’t placed here by accident.”

They moved further into the garden.

Suddenly, her steps slowed. "Hold on," she whispered, eyes narrowing. "Is that... a cigarette in his hand?"

Dr. Ade followed her gaze. There they were—three figures on the bench: the apostle, the man from Zimbabwe, and a younger man of North African descent sat in a quiet huddle. Smoke curled lazily into the air. A small pack of cigarettes lay between them. Members of staff stood nearby, sharing puffs of their own vapes and flavoured rolls. The garden had turned into a strange meeting ground.

"I thought he didn't smoke," the OT said, eyes wide. One hand moved slightly but remained tucked inside her pocket, as though holding herself back from marching over.

Dr. Ade gave a half-smile, already stepping forward.

"I told you," he said without looking back. "The man's full of surprises."

The scent of tobacco and sweet vape flavour mingled with the warm breeze as he approached the bench, curiosity rising in his chest like smoke itself.

THE YOUNG AND THE RESTLESS

Dr Ade stepped onto the soft gravel of the garden path, his polished shoes crunching beneath him as he walked towards the bench. The apostle sat still, his fingers gently cradling a perfectly rolled cigarette, its tip untouched by flame.

"Well, well," Dr Ade said with a crooked smile, his tone laced with playful sarcasm. "Are we smoking now, Apostle?"

Before the apostle could respond, the young Nigerian-British lad next to him leaned forward, voice sharp, eyes narrowed.

"Man's old enough to decide for himself. You can't keep treating people like kids," he said, his words cutting through the stillness like glass underfoot.

Dr Ade paused, keeping his posture calm. “Easy, brother! No one’s trying to take away his choices. Just caught me off guard, that’s all.”

The lad scoffed and turned to the man from Zimbabwe. “This is why I can’t stand this place.”

The Zimbabwean man, with legs crossed and shoulders relaxed, glanced at him sideways, voice low and smooth. “What’s the place done to you? Folks here treat you decently. I’ve seen it.”

The boy’s jaw clenched. He looked down at his hands, nails chewed to the quick. Then he looked up again, his voice cracking slightly.

“It’s not even about here,” he muttered. “It’s everything. My parents shoved me into this place because they didn’t want to deal with me. They’ve never listened—never tried to understand me.”

His foot tapped the ground in a restless rhythm. The words came quicker now, like a dam breaking.

“They say they love me, but only when I act like who they want me to be. Their love feels like a contract, with rules, conditions. If my dreams don’t mirror theirs, they don’t count. If my choices don’t fit into their perfect little plans, then suddenly I’m reckless. Ungrateful.”

His voice faded for a moment, then came back, softer, fragile.

“I know what I want. I’ve always known. But no one sees that.”

Silence settled like dust in the air. A breeze whispered through the garden, rustling the hedges nearby. Dr Ade's gaze dropped for a second, as though shielding himself from the boy's pain. The man from Zimbabwe didn't blink; he simply watched with the stillness of someone who's carried quiet grief for years.

The apostle hadn't moved, but the cigarette in his hand now trembled ever so slightly. His gaze was fixed on the boy, eyes unreadable.

"Who hurt you, son?" he asked, the words soft and without judgment.

The boy hesitated, his head lowering just a little. His fingers curled into the sleeves of his jumper. His lips parted, then closed again, as though weighing whether to speak. When he finally did, his voice barely made it past his throat.

"My parents," he said.

He turned his face slowly towards the apostle. The usual fire in his eyes had dulled, replaced with something cloudier, deeper. Like a storm sitting just beneath the surface, waiting to spill over. But he didn't cry. He just stared, face pale, as if the admission had taken more strength than he thought he had left.

None of the men spoke. The garden held its breath with them.

The boy spoke of broken and shattered dreams, of memories not made, of experiences not gained, of the nourishing scars left by his absent parents, of their constant quarrels and silent wars.

"I have been trudging down this hellish path for far too long, man, and it's tearing me apart, he growled, his eyes burning holes into the floor. I am tired of everyone trying to control my every move, telling me who I should be, and what I shouldn't do. It's maddening, man, it's draining every ounce of life from me" he complained as his eyes stared at the floor.

Next, they'll call you a rebel, a menace, when all you want is to be free from conformity, free from all these controls. It's gruelling, he quivered, his voice trembling, his fist clenched tight and his eyes flashing.

They tell you to follow your heart, yet when you do, they try to muzzle your voice. You seek only to speak your truth, to walk the path that burns brightest in your soul. They claim to know it all, but their lives are like hollow shells–echoing with the weight of conditioned thoughts, suffocating in the iron grip of outdated beliefs, and haunted by the ghosts of unresolved traumas.

No one said a word. They all turned their focus, hanging on every word. My parents were religious; yet their actions spoke volumes of darkness. They are the coldest-hearted people I've ever known. They have no feelings and are super insensitive, unloving, and uncaring.

They don't even love themselves, let alone others. In all the years I spent under their roof, granted to me only by social services, I saw nothing but power struggles. My father constantly fought to assert his dominance, believing it was his right to be revered as the head of the house–just as his ancestors were, or so he claimed. It was a battle for struggle, not for love.

His ideas were so traditional. Women are subordinate to men, and misogyny was an expression of love for him. How pathetic!

My mother, as the leader of this feminist movement, lived as a living embodiment, constantly aligning her actions with the ideals she advocated, and holding herself to the very standards of the system she tirelessly fought to shape and support.

To her ears, submission was synonymous with weakness. Allowing a man to take the lead felt like dropping your sword in the heat of battle–letting your enemies trample over you while you bowed at their feet, honouring them as if they were your conquerors.

Sometimes I would quietly approach the wall of their bedroom, hoping it would reveal the stories of their silent conflicts, the unspoken battles waged in their words. The walls, in their own way, shared how tension lingered even in their most intimate moments, I mean during sex.

My mother, a black British woman, lived by a code that made her see submission as a surrender of her feminist principles and self-respect. She preferred to be on top during sex, to assert her power–and in those moments, the dynamics of dominance and resistance seemed to take centre stage.

My father, an African man, with his toxic masculinity and misogynistic ideology and beliefs, would not allow that, because it would be a blow to his ego. According to him, a woman's rightful position is beneath him, and so it should be.

The wall once remarked that my mother often voiced her dissatisfaction, especially when it came to her relationship with my father. She felt that he was selfish, as his focus seemed only on his needs, with little concern for hers. Once he reached orgasm, it appeared as though he didn't care whether she was satisfied or not.

My mother, however, seemed unbothered by this dynamic. She had various personal items for her comfort, and I remembered when I was about ten years old, I found one of these items in her bag. I was curious and did not understand its purpose, so I began to play with it. It was mesmerising as I watched a rose-shaped toy vibrate, and I paid with my tears.

How vain and selfish they both were! They only lived for their egos. They didn't even care that I was always watching, damn adults! The boy bitterly complained, taking a long drag on the cigarette he held between his fingers.

The apostle listened spellbound as the young boy unleashed a torrent of raw emotion. Each word was a hammer strike, heavy with the unbearable weight of a tortured past, as his fury could shatter the chains of his childhood–a rusted, unyielding prison forged from neglect and unspeakable suffering.

"But you will grow up one day. You know, you are 21. Isn't that already adulthood?" the apostle asked him.

"Well, at least I am not an uptight adult like they are, and I never will be. Why do you think I am fighting for my freedom? To think differently and not be ruled by mere ideas created by humans in this godforsaken system we live and die in.

I want out of the matrix that my ignorant parents were ruled by. That's all I am for; that's all I stand for. But what do I get for trying to think for myself? Do you want me to be confined here, be fed psychoactive drugs, and reduced to mere labels and profiles like a ghost, drifting through life without substance or voice? All I want is to be free and be me," the boy replied soberly, releasing the half-burnt cigarette from the firm grip of his fingers, between which it was stuck.

As the cigarette kissed the ground, tiny silver tears rolled down his cheeks from his left eye, which he wiped away almost instantly as he stepped on the cigarette to put it out. "Strong men show no emotion; only weak men cry," he said, snorting and glaring at the Zimbabwean standing next to the apostle.

"I know I can't say I know how you feel, but I know what it means to yearn to be free. I was once a youngster like you, but the question in my mind was always, 'Can you be free?' Mine wasn't to be free from my parents. They were great people and quite wealthy, so I can't complain. But I wanted to be free from always wanting more.

My parents always wanted more; they would do anything to make sure they made more money. You are valued only if you are an elite. Money was the god we prayed to because it answered all our prayers. But here I am now, in my 60s, still wishing and still worshipping. So, it's not just a youth or adult thing; I think everyone wants to be free.

What do you think about this, apostle? What is your understanding of being free? Are you also in search of freedom? Well, it's obvious that you're, otherwise you wouldn't be locked up in this madhouse like the rest of us," the man from Zimbabwe said sarcastically and smiled. "But you know what I mean — what is your idea of freedom? Tell us about freedom," the man asked the apostle.

The apostle sat quietly, his fingers brushing against the grass as if he were reading the earth. His eyes, dark and steady, gazed into nothing and everything all at once. A faint breeze stirred the trees, whispering through the open sky like a secret no one could keep. He slowly lifted his head, his voice calm but heavy with meaning.

"Deep in the heart of Africa lies a captivating and verdant treasure, a glorious dense forest teeming with life and endowed with the most beautiful trees. Its lush canopy stretched as far as the eye could see, and the legs could trudge, providing a haven for diverse flora and fauna. The sun's rays dance through the dense foliage while the wind whistles through the space, creating a breathtaking carpet of light and shade," the apostle replied and kept speaking.

"In the same forest, there lived a bird named Saqqara, with feathers as elegant and golden as the 7 am sun in Marrakesh.

With its wingspan so broad and its weight so dense, Saqqara spent its moments perched firmly on the branch of the baobab tree rooted in the heart of the forest, gazing at the sky. But something troubled Saqqara's heart, a deep conviction that the sky was nothing more than a cage and soaring therein was the death of his freedom. Saqqara wanted to prove the other birds wrong. They said he wasn't bold enough. So, out of rebellion, he flapped his wings and tried to fly. But each time, something unseen held him back.

He peered through the mental bars that stood like tree stumps and stared at other birds gliding freely as their wings were caressed by the wind. The longing for release grew in Saqqara, a pain that filled his every breath, the misery that set the pace of his heartbeat.

One day, a bird suddenly perched near Saqqara. It was as if it were his reflection, only older and weathered. Who are you? Saqqara asked. I am your higher self," replied the old bird.

Why do you remain trapped in these imaginary bars? asked the old bird. The sky is wide, an open canvas waiting for your flight. Saqqara tilted his head, confused. But don't you see the bars, old friend? They surround me and hold me back.

The old bird smiled gently. The bars are only alive in your head, Saqqara. You are the master of your cage. Open your eyes and spread your wings, and you will discover that the sky was never a cage but a boundless sanctuary.

Just like Saqqara, I ask you, my beloved, who told you that you were bound, imprisoned, and put in a box? Wouldn't believing that you are not free make you a prisoner of your demise? You are constantly waging wars against yourself to free yourself, forgetting that the very idea of fighting for freedom is a sophisticated affirmation and acceptance of your lack of freedom. It takes a slave to seek freedom. Release can only be sought by those who are bound.

Can air, in all its warmth, cry out for freedom or go to war with itself when it is trapped within the confines of an inflated balloon? It is aware that it cannot be bound, no matter how big the balloon is or how long it stays inflated. It thrives in the moment, understanding that its very presence in the balloon is what gives it essence and purpose.

Verily, you are breath, and in the world of form, your body is the balloon. Of what value is the body without breath?

If the breath believes it is imprisoned within the body and desperately seeks to break free, wouldn't its very purpose cease to exist if it finally achieves freedom?

The wise man, deeply attuned to his true essence and origin, does not wage war against himself. Instead, he rests in the divinity of his liberation, grounded in love and life.

Verily, I say to you, rebellion has never set a soul free. Instead, it binds the soul, transforming it into the very force it seeks to oppose.

Freedom is indeed the bright sun at the peak; love is the steady flame that leads the way.

Why fight for freedom when its very essence resides within you? When love is the force that guides your soul, it becomes the unwavering light that dispels every shadow, even the darkest ones woven by the illusion of limitation. The soul that is anchored in love knows no fear, for it is beyond the reach of ego and mental enslavement. So, I beseech you, do not seek freedom, for it is already yours, inherent in your very being. Love in this awareness, and watch your soul erupt, unfolding in its boundless, true essence.

So, I ask you again, my son: who has ensnared you in this web of false beliefs? Who has twisted your mind and convinced you that your very existence hinges on an unending battle for freedom?" The apostle's voice rang out with fervent conviction, burning with a passionate intensity. "Who has shackled your thoughts and led you to believe that this struggle for freedom is your sole purpose in life?"

"But isn't that what it is? My parents, who are Christians, have always said that you can only be free in this evil and terrible world if you are like Christ, and if you are not like Christ, you are a slave to the world," the boy replied.

"I grew up in that faith too, because that was all the priests taught in Sunday school when I was young," Dr. Ade said, leaning against the wall, close to the apostle.

"Can a man in fetters and manacles set another free by giving them the keys to unlock their shackles?" the apostle asked, turning to the young lad and swiftly turning again to face Doctor Ade. "Yet, your parents and priests claimed to have given you the keys to set you free from the world and all of its pains. How free are they that love is suffocated in their presence, and peace is a stranger to their soul?

If you become like Christ, as they beseech you to be, who then will you be you? Wouldn't it be a profound waste of God's divine creation, the universal mind, and divine intelligence to create, only for you to deny your true self? How can you ever bind and imprison your essence in false beliefs, thinking that by imitating the Saviour, you can somehow become free, perfect, and whole?

Aye, your preachers will say that man has erred, yet to embody the saviour is the divine blueprint–the very essence of what God envisions humanity to become: free, whole, and transcendent.

But I ask you, as I asked your fathers: What perfect God creates imperfections? What God, who is freedom itself, has as its reflection a God in Gyves, Darbies, and Bilboes, just so that his reflection can be freed from its chains by the act of being something other than God itself?

A soul is only as free as the knowledge of itself is, for a king who is unaware of his kingship calls his throne a quod. If you don't know who you are, someone else will convince you to be who you are not. Only a mind drowning in the pool of bondage believes it needs freedom.

If a fish sees the sea as its cage because it thinks the crocodile that goes ashore is free, it will only meet its death at the gate of its freedom. A fish that knows that its freedom lies in the presence of its fins does not need to fight with the water.

Aye, your cage is the mental limitation placed on yourself through your perception of yourself. If you can break free from the thought of being bound, only then will you truly be free. But if it is necessary to fight or rebel, then let your rebellion have a divine reason.

Fight to be yourself, and rebel against the thoughts and beliefs that condition you to think that you are bound. Let love be your weapon of rebellion, let peace be your shield, and let your total belief in yourself and the God within you be the horse you ride into war against mental slavery.

No one can bind you, enslave you, or take away your freedom until you surrender it to them by believing and being something other than yourself. You are life itself, experiencing the world through a human lens.

HOPE
HOPE
HOPE
HOPE
HOP
HOP
HOPE
HOPE

HOPE FOR SALE

The sun burned like a golden crown and shed its glowing rays while the heat continued unabated. It was 3 P.M, and the apostle was still holding his cigarette in between his fingers, unlit.

“I know you didn’t want to smoke that,” scoffed Dr. Ade with a sardonic smile on his face. “Maybe, maybe not. To be honest, it feels much better between my fingers than on my lips,” replied the apostle.

Just as Dr. Ade began to speak again, he was interrupted by another British-born Nigerian in his late 20s named Chris. He was known for his constant philosophical and religious arguments on the ward, often with himself or with other residents, always shouting that he was the new messiah and the facility was the Vatican. He was diagnosed with paranoid schizophrenia and hyper-religiosity.

Chris, standing six paces away from the young Nigerian, the apostle, Dr. Ade, and the man from Zimbabwe, walked towards them. He took a tentative step forward while clutching the book he would never put down tightly to his chest.

The conversations in the hall and now in the garden had given him a taste of the old man's knowledge, and he had come to believe that the apostle had the answers to the burning questions that had plagued his curious, schizoid mind.

Chris approached the apostle, his eyes full of amazement and uncertainty. The apostle tilted his head; his face marked by dark wisdom and lived experience. He smiled kindly, the corners of his eyes sparkling, giving Chris a subtle sign to put aside his fears and speak.

"Are you well, my son?" the apostle asked in a calm tone. "Why are whirlwinds of unspoken words and unanswered questions dancing through the corridors of your mind?

Chris took a deep breath to calm his anxieties. "Sir, I overheard everything you said from the beginning of the event to this very second. You said a few moments ago that there was no freedom to pursue, which was clear to me. But I wonder if there is a need to save if there is no freedom to pursue.

Does that mean that the stories of Jesus and other prophets are just fabrications? What place do prophets, saviours, and I, as the messiah, have in the scheme of things? From my research, it appears that the core of their teachings as saviours and prophets is freedom, both spiritual and mental."

The apostle's gaze turned distant, as if he were looking into the depths of his memories. His voice, when he spoke again, was filled with a mixture of melancholy and realisation.

"Aye, the tales told by moonlight, the story of the carpenter's son, the saviour from Bethlehem, and the prophet from Mecca, is a tale as old as time itself."

"True to their word," the apostle continued, "the beauty of life lies in the stories we tell, the truths we discover in them, the lessons we learn on our journey, and how much we use those lessons as instruments to carve, create, experience, and express life." Chris scowled, not entirely satisfied with the apostle's answer. "But, sir, I need to know if it's true. Did these prophets exist? Are their messages genuine?"

The apostle nodded a deep understanding evident in his eyes. "Exactly, my young man" The strength of stories lies not in their veracity but in the truths and teachings they convey and how they help you remember who you are.

Whether Jesus lived on earth or not, whether your prophets and saviours existed or not, whether they are true or not, their stories have inspired generosity, compassion, and a longing for a better life to experience and express it. And that is of great value because hope is sold the way it should be sold.

Chris' doubts began to fade and were replaced by a new understanding of the complexity of reality. "I appreciate that, sir," he said, staring at the apostle as the others all stood, listening more and talking less.

"Well, I think I get it. The goal is to find meaning and inspiration in the stories we come across, not to prove or disprove them. But what exactly do you mean when you say that hope is sold as it should be?" He asked the apostle.

The apostle asks him in reply, What is hope, if not the very stem that serves as the scaffolding upon which the leaves and fruits thrive? It is the tree's spine—the source of stability, veracity and vitality from which its life expression and experience flourish and bear fruit.

Have you not been told that you are the tree of life? How alive can your life be and feel if it is drained of hope?

Hope is the late September breeze that caresses the sails of our daydreams and blows them to distant horizons. It is the spark that burns brightly amidst the ruins of our shattered doubts. We weave possibilities, desires, and magic by grasping its ethereal threads, our hearts serving as the needle with which we stitch our desires with our eyes closed, opening them to the reality of our dreams.

The eagle wakes up and spreads its wings to soar as high into the air as its lungs can carry it. It hopes that the belief in the love it shares with the sky will not let go of it, no matter how dark and stormy the sky, no matter how blue its face.

The lion wakes with hope in its heart, its mind free from limits and its hunger boundless. With purposeful steps, it roams the jungle, trusting that fate will guide it to its prey and direct its energy where it's meant to go.

"Hope, I say to you, is the salt of existence," the apostle continued, "but in the world ruled by merchants, everything is a commodity, and unfortunately, hope is the most coveted."

"To children, the merchants peddle dreams wrapped in the guise of a bright future, promising them the title of 'leaders of tomorrow.' Yet, beneath this facade, they create a hellish prison, a turmoil-laden cell, manipulating innocence to boost the insatiable demand for their wares. In a twisted game of commerce, the hope they sell becomes a torment, driving a desperate hunger for something they can never truly possess."

To the unsuspecting teenager, the merchant hawks the seductive illusion of freedom, sparkling brightly at the age of 18. Yet, if only the youth could pierce the veil of deception, they would see that the freedom promised is but a mirage, a tantalising dream that evaporates upon closer inspection.

Instead of liberation, it leaves the spirit raw and exposed, like a fragile chrysalis torn asunder, bruised and battered, cast aside as if it were nothing more than a discarded remnant of hope.

To the soul that finds comfort in lecture halls, the merchant offers the enticing hope of a brighter tomorrow through the skills of reading, writing, and speaking. But what if this soul could realise that true understanding comes from grasping time and its natural laws? This wisdom isn't taught in classrooms; it shows that the merchant's goods are pointless.

A better tomorrow isn't built on empty promises and fancy words; it comes from being aware of what's needed in every moment of life. Tomorrow and the future are just a series of present moments seen through the eyes of mental binoculars.

To the beaten and broken, to the poor and hungry, the merchant offers a mirage of a golden chest buried in a grand mansion, demanding their humility and meekness as payment.

The downtrodden remain trapped in a purgatory, longing for a refuge built from the ashes of hollow promises and fading hopes.

To the man who has condemned himself, the merchant offers the hope of Nirvana, found in the lotus that blooms amid chaos. Its petals symbolise silence, and its fragrance brings peace to the doves. If only the man knew that nirvana exists in everything that breathes and that there's no cost to reach it.

If only he realised that what the merchant sells is just a distraction, preventing him from looking within. In remembering, those who have condemned themselves will discover the calm shores of the sea that leads to Nirvana.

To the people whose land trembles under the weight of conflict and tremor, under the vendetta against happiness, safety, and free living, the merchant sells hope in a chariot full of pipe dreams driven by utopian promises. The merchant sells hope to the lost soul, offering maps that will lead them home.

Yet, these maps lead the soul further away, in search of a mirage known as the long road home. The more the soul thinks it is approaching self-knowledge by following the map, the more it drifts away from its true self. This highlights a cruel twist of fate. Seeking the way home only takes it further from where it truly belongs.

For a heart that craves companionship like a beggar seeks charity, sadness echoes in its heartbeat, and loneliness shapes its rhythm. The merchant views these hearts as travellers longing for connection. Where can love be found if not in the home built by hope? "Buy as much hope as you desire," cries the merchant. He offers hope to those mourning lost love and aching for what is out of reach. Yet, the heart that feels alone may mistake this loneliness, meant to reveal the divine presence of God, as eternal damnation.

Verily, hope is the essence of breath. Breath, as I taught your fathers, is life. It is the beat of our sultry wings against the firm grip of fate. Embrace it with all your might, for in this fleeting dance of being, we illuminate life with possibility, pushing back the ego and finding meaning in the present and all it has to offer.

"Therefore, I exhort you to deal carefully with every merchant you meet at this fair you call existence, with the consciousness that hope is not in the products sold to you in the form of ideas, rules, beliefs, trends, and illusory blueprints, but in the hearts of those to whom the goods are sold," said the apostle.

No one spoke a word as the apostle finished his speech. Yet, his words cast a soothing glow on all the hearts that listened to him as he spoke.

Chris was speechless, his eyes glued to the apostle, captivated by the profound wisdom the schizophrenic old man had just imparted to him. This is so much to carry, he said to the apostle.

"Well, I have said nothing new. I have only reminded you of the truth in you that you are already aware of," the apostle replied.

"But why are you here?" Chris asked again. "This is a madhouse for us who have been labelled crazy, and yes, I know you do not belong here. I have this strong feeling. My intuition has never led me astray, I am sure of what I feel, and the feeling is that there's a mix-up somewhere. So tell me, why are you here?"

The atmosphere suddenly became quiet, and everyone was ready at that moment to hear the answer the apostle was about to give. Buried deep in the minds of all who had heard him speak since they had entered the garden were the same questions Chris had boldly asked.

And like the tender embrace of fire and water, which was his answer to their highly expectant hearts, the apostle calmly replied, "Are we not all insane?"

Disappointment hung heavy, expectations shattered, and hope dashed. How can he ask a question in response to the question he was asked? Dr Ade thought to himself as he stood staring at the apostle.

When Chris wanted to speak during the silence, the occupational therapist who was moderating the event came into the garden and yelled softly with a worried look: "Are you lads going to miss the second part of this great event? The rest of the event will continue inside. Let's go into the hall where we can continue to chat and enjoy each other's company."

Some of the patients reluctantly extinguished their cigarettes and made their way into the apartment and down the hall, while the others, including Dr. Ade, accompanied the apostle as they left the garden and went into the building.

STAGNANT WATERS AND EMPTY VESSELS

The occupational therapist, a beacon of warmth, stood before the crowd in the auditorium, her kind eyes like gentle lanterns illuminating the eager faces around her. The air buzzed with the electric energy of conversation, laughter weaving through the throng as people filled the hall, the rhythmic creaking of chairs echoing like a chorus of anticipation.

With a deep, fortifying breath that seemed to gather the very essence of the moment, she straightened her outfit—a subtle gesture signifying readiness. Her watch glinted in the soft light, a silent reminder that time waits for no one. As the clock struck the appointed hour, she clapped her hands twice, a crisp sound that sliced through the chatter and summoned attention like a conductor raising a baton. With a wave of her presence, the patients and staff gradually quietened, their rapt gazes drawn to her as if she were an enchanting storyteller poised to share a great adventure.

"Welcome back to the second act of this remarkable psychotherapeutic journey!" the occupational therapist proclaimed, her voice a harmonious blend of professionalism and friendliness, resonating like a soothing melody in the hearts of those gathered. "I hope you all had a refreshing smoke break," she asked, her tone laced with playful curiosity.

"Well, I am truly delighted, and I know you are too," she continued, a grin blooming on her face like a bright flower. "There are a myriad of activities waiting for us, each one a stepping stone toward understanding and connection, so let us dive in!"

"You can speak your mind at any moment," she encouraged, her words like an open invitation to a dance of dialogue. "The aim of today, as we all know, is to draw from the well of each other's experiences, to share stories that ripple through our lives and create waves of understanding."

"The aim of today, as we all know, is to learn from each other's experiences. In this zone, there are no judgments and no wrong or right questions, so do not worry.

The apostle, as he is affectionately called—although he claims to be nameless," she said, smiling sarcastically, "will continue to share his profound knowledge and experience," she added, staring at the apostle, who replied with a beaming smile hidden under his thick beard.

In the far corner of the room, where the sunlight no longer reached, sat the elderly Sudanese woman in her wheelchair, almost tucked into the shadows. A soft humming sound came from her direction, a quiet tune with no words, just the low vibration of a memory. The two overstuffed bags hanging from her chair brushed against her sides with every small movement, like faithful companions who had followed her through decades.

Silver strands laced through her long, dark hair, which hung loose and fell across her shoulders. Her eyes wandered the room, not really seeing, not really searching, just floating between the present and somewhere far off. Her hands gripped the fabric of one bag tightly, fingers twitching now and then as if counting invisible things.

She hadn't spoken during the first part of the session. She simply sat there, blinking slowly. Her body was still, except for the occasional, faint shift.

She unravelled her demented thoughts like a tangled thread and rolled her wheelchair a little further so that the apostle could hear her. Her eyes reflected confusion and vulnerability, but her question was profound.

"How do we navigate the labyrinth of attachment and avariciousness?" she asked. "Since tomorrow isn't promised, what use will it be to let go of that which I have, knowing I might not have another if I lose this one that I own?"

"What I regret are the ideas I had but never realised," she said with her head bowed in shame, "and the things I never needed but from which I always drew life. Talk to me about letting go, sir. Was it selfish to hoard the things I had? Is it wise to keep things for yourself and never let them go? Isn't it wise to keep things, even if they are old, because who knows if you will need them tomorrow?"

All was silent again as the apostle leaned forward and began to speak.

"Imagine a beautiful mosaic woven with threads of ego-induced attachments and hoardings. At first glance, it looks like heaven, but if you look closer, you can see the intricate knots that are limiting you. Hoarding plunders your contentment like a ravenous beast because you cling to the illusion of permanence.

Incessantly, you have been taught by your teachers and prophets to take as much as you can carry and to save for rainy days. Yet, they have forgotten to teach the most important thing. Isn't every day a rainy day? Isn't every moment full of challenges to be overcome and souls to be blessed?

How much can your heart bear, and how much can your soul carry when the mind clings to all things and never lets anything go? So much knowledge have you gained, so much wealth have you amassed, so many ideas have you locked up within, for fear of loss and uncertainty.

How trivial it is to stockpile ideas meant for summer for fear of running out of them when winter comes.

Doesn't the source of warmth nourish the tree even as it sheds its leaves, providing comfort in the summer when the sun is quietly resting during winter?

Doesn't the source of heat give warmth to the tree when it needs it? What purpose would spring serve if the tree clung to its leaves in autumn, fearing that releasing them would invite the harsh chill of winter?

How obsolete will such a hoarded idea be when the cold hand of winter craves a warm embrace? How irrelevant will such suppressed creativity and amassed possessions be when death calls? Like stagnant water will thy soul be, for every idea hoarded only serves as a dam obstructing life's flow. Hence, it becomes still water, albeit a trash can, taking in so much but giving out nothing.

The flow of life is trapped in a sludge of inactivity, in stagnant waters that reflect the mirror image of a clouded soul. There, possibilities trickle away like swift waves, while ambitions wither in the suffocating grip of the soul's rigidity.

The symphony of life and its melodious tune ends in stagnation, leaving a desolate echo that haunts the ego-dominated mind. Why would such a soul not stay stagnated?

The energy within it is obstructed because of the dams and impediments created by ego-driven ideas, low-vibration self-perceptions, and viewpoints that are attached to it but were never dropped. They were never unlearnt when it was time for new experiences.

Imagine a lung that inhales endlessly, yet never exhales. What remains of it is but a burden of stagnation? Similarly, consider a vessel that voraciously absorbs energy without creating an outlet. Such a vessel cannot endure; its unchecked intake will ultimately lead to ruin. In the same way, lungs that fail to exhale will be overwhelmed and crushed by the weight of inertia. Both serve as stark reminders of the necessity for balance—of giving and receiving, of inhaling and exhaling. Without this equilibrium, life succumbs to collapse.

Have you not been taught that still water has no current? Can a ship be propelled without energy or current flowing in and through it? Can a soul function without breath when the current flows in but has no way out of its lungs? Like a river trapped, choked by stagnation, it cannot thrive.

Breath is not just life; it is the vital rhythm that sustains the spirit. Without release, the soul suffocates, withering in the silence of unexpressed vitality. Why do you obstruct the flow of life within you by always hoarding and never letting go?

If the sky withheld its rain, if the sun kept back its warmth, and if the trees denied their fruit and leaves, what would remain? We would be left in a barren world, aching for nature's gifts, lost in a silence that tells of all we need to thrive.

Unfortunately, adulthood has turned your soul from a blank slate into stagnant water, shaped by the ideas and truths handed to you by society.

Everything is perceived as a trophy: ideas, possessions, traumas. Everything that should be experienced and dropped has become bricks and sticks, which your soul has used to build walls and dams. These promote stagnation and hinder the flow of energy," said the apostle.

The Sudanese woman listened attentively, her heart heavy with realisation. "And what about attachments?" she asked soberly.

"Attachments," the apostle replied, "masquerade as love, but they have the power to limit and prevent us from seeing the beauty of impermanence. We cling to transitory ideas, events, and things to feel comfortable about the past or future. But in doing this, we miss the true meaning of the present moment. I implore you to stop clinging to your life and let it flow freely, like a cloud moved by the wind. Only then can your soul live and experience total fulfilment in existence."

The woman thought about his words for a few seconds. "But letting go is hard," she admitted.

"It is indeed," the apostle acknowledged. "This is the beauty and fun of existence. It is the act of breathing in and out, the divine art and act of birth and death, of thought and creation, of seed and harvest times; all of which represent the flow of energy and life itself.

But like golden autumn leaves that fall gracefully, let go of what no longer serves you. Feel free to express ideas and creativity without fear or ego-inspired limitations, because your source of inspiration is unlimited.

Aim to be an empty vessel, free from attachment to dead things, moments, and ideas. Itt is the empty vessels that are most valued and utilised in life. The flow of energy can only fill empty vessels. Their emptiness is proof of their vitality and unhindered flow of energy. So, be an adult with the mind of a child.

The child is an empty vessel, always creating, always letting go, and always in the moment. Be an empty vessel; I urge you again as I urged your fathers, prophets, and teachers.

For in this emptiness, you will discover the space to fill your soul with that which is essential, such as love, joy, peace, and the profound beauty of the ever-changing universe. The tighter you hold on to life and do not let go when change calls, the deeper you sink into utter delusion and lose sight of what is real and the true essence of life.

Only when you accept and embrace the divine, ephemeral nature of life can you set yourself free. By letting go, you create a space in which the soul can blossom majestically, unbound, wild, free, and born again momentarily," said the apostle.

His words echoed and left a whiff of wisdom in the air. The Sudanese lady felt a certain peace rise within her, like rays of sunlight shining through a torn veil, and for the first time in a long time, the member of staff supporting her saw her smile. Indeed, the truth itself is an ecstasy, she thought to herself.

DEAD MINDS, LOVERS, AND SOULS MADE OF STONE

On the far-right side of the hall, pressed against the cold white wall like a shadow, the young Moroccan woman stood still, her body drawn tight like a bowstring. Her arms were folded tightly across her chest, knuckles white.

The thick paperback she always carried—its cover worn, corners bent—was wedged beneath her armpit, pages slightly open, as if even the book had grown tired of waiting to be read.

She said nothing. She never did, not until she had something to say.

Her head hung low, dark curls brushing her cheek, but her eyes never left the Apostle. She watched him as if she could peel back each word, as if the shape of his mouth was hiding answers she had been denied.

She stood like that for most of the session—frozen, yet buzzing inside. Her crossed ankles shifted slightly, toes tapping to a rhythm only she could hear. There was a quiet intensity to her, like a candle flickering in a locked room where no one else could breathe the same air.

"I long for truth in all matters of the heart, but the fear of vulnerability that change brings is like a shackle to my soul. There's never a shortage of alms in the pockets of givers, they say, but you know that's a false narrative because people never stop taking until you are drained and then left for dead. Will the passion and fervour of love fade away like the quicksand of the Erg Chebbi dunes in Merzouga slipping through my fingers?

The walls I have built, stronger and higher than those of China, have done their job so that thieves cannot plunder my soul and my happiness, but they have also blocked my view; I can hardly see reality," she said dolorously.

Like a delicate pendulum, her heart swung back and forth between turmoil and serenity as she continued to lament.

She flitted through the labyrinth of love like an injured bird perched anxiously on brittle limbs. Trust, like a delicate blossom, wilted in the twilight of fear that blackened the walls of her heart. Her emotional compass whirled and got lost in the maelstrom, while the symphony of her soul searched for harmony in the dissonance of change.

The apostle, a beacon of empathy, is seated like a lighthouse, ready to illuminate the way for a ship battling the stormy sea.

"Why do you live as if your heart were made of stone?" he asked her in reply.

"Fear has become the chisel with which your reality is shaped so that your soul hardly realises that it is more resilient than being broken and unloved. Its nature knows no limit, and the wind of change never blows against it, for its essence aligns perfectly with the purpose of the soul. Just as the wind flows freely, so does it embody that same spirit.

The freedom of love is like the wind, my dear. It is everywhere you go. Your experience of it hinges on your awareness of its presence. But how can a soul be conscious if its eyes are widely closed? How can your soul experience love when it is so afraid to express itself?

Have you not been taught by your teachers and prophets that what you give comes back to you and that what you can experience depends on how much you are willing to express?

How can a soul feel alive when it is not living? How can you receive love when you are barely sharing love? How can you be present when you can't feel? How can you perceive when you can barely see?

What makes your soul needy, even in all its eternal fullness, if not sheer humanity? What numbs your soul of breath and all that it is, if not fear the consecrated price you have to pay for unawareness?

Like a winter fog, fear wraps its frosty claws around your soul and hinders its vibrant rhythm. It darkens your dreams, clogs your heart, and interrupts the flow of passion and life so deeply that the beats of your heart, which were gratifying and joyful, fade into a haunting ultrasound. The sleep that used to be adorned with sweet dreams now shares its bed with nightmares, and your waking days full of daydreams are now shrouded in a thick fog of fear and anxiety.

Aye, fear as alchemy transforms the soul, once bright and blue as the summer sky, into a barren night sky at 2 a.m. It fills the soul with confusion and despair, destroying the shooting and twinkling stars that once illuminated the path to self-awareness.

Inspired by fear, you have perfectly erected walls to secure that which you have but don't own. An experience that, by its essence, knows no boundaries, your walls have given parameters to.

Verily, I say to you, a soul is dead that doesn't share for fear of its well running empty. And the most miserable of souls is the one that perceives its source as limited.

But I ask you, what are you really afraid of? Is it your heart breaking, or are your expectations being shattered like broken glasses on marble floors?" The apostle asked.

The Moroccan woman inhaled deeply, letting the breath linger before slowly releasing it in a long exhale. Silence stretched between them, but after a few moments, her lips parted, revealing what her heart had been holding back all along.

"Do I love right? Or is it not intended for a black woman like me to be truly loved for who I am and not for what I am?" she asked bitterly.

"In all honesty, apostle, I carry the weight of grief in the quiet crevices of my mind. The butterflies in my stomach that once danced to the symphony of love within me with the promise of hope, charm, and optimism now feel dead.

Repeatedly, my soul has opened up to embrace love and all its marvellous tidings, only to cradle broken dreams and vain promises. Each scar it bears is a faded echo of my undying love, a mosaic of passion for life left behind. The sands of time have indeed flowed through my fingers, leaving me with a handful of nostalgic memories and painful regrets as souvenirs. The embrace of love has now turned to misery, and I am constantly writing stories of loss and anger in my head like ink on papyrus.

"So, tell me, why shouldn't I, like other broken Black women, build walls as thick as the hurt within me?

Why shouldn't I doubt or fear love when it approaches the gates of my soul?" she asked the apostle, despondently.

"I do resonate and empathise with your pain and grief, my dear," the apostle answered heartily. "But then, it seems to me so lugubrious and amazingly poignant how much strength and vigour humans employ just to clone a once jaunty, effervescent, and chirpy self into a harsh-looking, bitter, and misery-stricken self, all in a bid to perfectly conceal their fragile loving hearts.

You were created to love; there is no escape from it. You were created to share, for if you do not share, you will become clogged. How lifeless the body becomes when it is tamed to be unfeeling. How much have you been indoctrinated—to the point of believing—that true self-awareness and self-control are about numbing the raw, uncomfortable pain you fear, and desperately chasing only the emotions you've been conditioned to crave?

Aye, I tell you as I told your fathers. Happiness, sorrow, joy, anger, pain, depression, grief, highs, lows, boredom, laughter, and the likes are all different fruits of the same tree. The tree of life has a bark made of feelings, and its trunk supports the fruits that grow from it.

Aye, it is peace of mind to feel angry, it is peace of mind to cry, for all has one thing as its essence: feeling.

Therefore, it is the core of emotional intelligence to feel and divine self-control to express what one feels correctly. Emotional intelligence is the living essence of the Holy Spirit, a divine spark that ignites our hearts with wisdom and empathy. It whispers to us in moments of doubt, guiding our connections and illuminating the path of understanding. Embrace it, for it is the sacred dance of our souls. The divine art of willing it right in love and through love momentarily is the eternal act of self-mastery.

But how can one be emotionally intelligent if one chooses feelings that evoke only happiness and laughter and numbs the painful feelings?

Can a tree choose to embrace only the youth and splendour of summer, shedding its leaves to numb itself to the harshness of winter—the pain, starkness, and piercing cold?

Yet, being a tree, it understands that while winter strips away everything it knows and loves, leaving it exposed and bare, there is an emotional depth in that experience. This doesn't mean it will shut itself off from feeling the coldness of winter, as that would deny it the joy of being reborn in spring and the beauty of experiencing the vibrant energy of summer.

You shout that you love yourself, forgetting that the backbone of love is self-knowledge. Are you not aware that feeling is the essential key that unlocks the door to self-discovery? Then, how can you love a self that cannot feel? How can you be aware of what you cannot feel?

Isn't self-awareness the ability to fully experience life in all its facets in an instant, free from evaluation, numbness, or suppression?

How much have these hopefuls seduced you into being an expert at numbing life and thus becoming a profound and super-creative emotional civil engineer, erecting walls as tall as towers in Babel?

When the feelings you experience are shrouded in a heavy cloak of pain, you cast them aside, bind them tightly, and pour your desperate prayers over them, hoping to silence their haunting echoes. When they come in a long, flowing garment of joy, you give thanks for them and pray for their permanence and eternal repetition. They become ignorant of the divine truth that both visitors under the garments are the same. To deny one is to deny the other, and to accept one is to accept the established order.

Were you not taught that love is pain and peace is war? Did your fathers not teach you that happiness is sorrow, and seeking wealth is proof of the presence of poverty? Or do you not know that the presence of God is a refined proof of the devil, and that light is darkness in a brighter tone?

You wear barbed wire around your heart like tree bark to prick the hands that dare to feel its rhythmic beat, and yet you complain that your heart bleeds. Do you not know that emotional stagnation is also self-harm? How shallow are the depths of such a soul? How pathetic is its calibre?

Have you not heard how deadly the surface of stagnant water is? Yet, you laboriously turn the springs that flow within you into swamps, with ideas, rules, labels, and titles.

Do you not realise that to truly express and feel love, all it takes is to let the currents of life flow freely within you and around you? To deny yourself the expression and experience of love is like constructing dams against a flowing river of life, stifling its vitality and depriving it of the freedom to nourish and enrich every soul it encounters. To erect barriers against the water that symbolises the essence of life is to suffocate its flow, robbing it of the natural spontaneity that allows it to grace and rejuvenate every soul it touches.

The appealing charm and ingrained norms of the cultures that shape your ego create a false illusion. This blinds you to the deeper harmonies beyond your understanding and leads you to accept their narrow ideas of love, mistaking one note for the whole orchestra of existence.

Conversely, you have made these illusions your staple diet when your belly growls for an expression of love and your soul thirsts for its experience. You curse and revile the same source from which you draw living water. The sand beneath your feet that gives your foot a foothold, you call common and praise it only when you use it, then spit and step on it when it has lost its value and its job is done.

Is it not said that one should love like this? If there is no certainty, then the mood is dead. How puzzling it is, in a world where all living things have such a short life, to want to see the future of love before removing the obstacles that weigh down the heart.

If all that love can do is live in a moment, why not express and experience it when it is alive instead of mourning it when it is dead?"

"So, I urge you, dear lovers," the apostle declared, standing up, "with your closed minds and hardened hearts, to truly feel—

feel deeply and never stop. Because to feel is to truly live, and to live is to love.

"As you embrace your feelings, change will inevitably emerge, often accompanied by pain. But remember this: art may shatter, yet it always has the power to heal. Love is art. It has no rules, no name, no future, and no past. It exists solely in the present moment, defined by its expression and shaped by its experiences.

Living means letting it flow, and letting it flow means resisting the urge to tame it, name it, or label it. "As you boldly embrace the journey of life, strive to surround yourself with those who ignite the best within you. Allow them to dwell tenderly in your heart. Yet, be vigilant: let those who bring forth your shadows reside in the same house as your heart, but keep them at a distance, for their presence should serve as a reminder of the strength you possess to rise above."

The apostle's words felt like balls of fire, slowly melting the ice of doubt, rigidity and emotional stagnation that surrounded the Moroccan woman's heart. Words that had such a calming effect on the soul and yet, like a vault, her heart needed even more conviction to break through the locks.

Still appalled by what the apostle was saying, she moved a few steps away from where she had been standing and walked closer to the apostle, while everyone stared without saying a word.

She looked at him for a few seconds and asked, "What if I dismantle these walls that have been the buffer of my fragile heart for years and let someone in who ends up taking everything my soul owns and never replenishing it?

The fragility and susceptibility that go hand in hand with vulnerability seem to me like teetering on the edge of a slippery slope, taking a risk, yet being careful lest I fall into the abyss. Besides, people are unpredictable, and when we reveal our true selves, the nakedness of our souls, and the sincerity of our hearts, we only take-home suffering and pain as souvenirs.

The apostle calmly walked up to her, placed his left palm on her shoulder, and turned to face the rest of the audience while addressing her question.

We are all like her, he said, pointing his right finger at the audience. You, you, you, and even I—no one is left out. We all move through life with the hopeful belief that the love we share makes us whole and will never leave us feeling empty. For each of us, being hollow feels like a deep loss, as if our worth has slipped away.

I beseech you, therefore, to hold this truth close to your heart: love has the power to bind us together, yet it can also tear us apart. This beautiful act of love wasn't meant to fill you up and make you whole; it was crafted in its divine essence to redefine you, to strip away what no longer serves you, and to illuminate the emptiness that can lead to profound growth. Yet, you've been led to believe that love is meant to complete you, filling your gaps and mending your wounds. This notion has been ingrained in you, shaping your understanding of love as a source of wholeness.

Don't you see that the endless quest for wholeness is a clear reflection of your sense of brokenness, your fragmented self, and your feelings of incompleteness? It serves as a reminder of the parts of you that feel unhealed and unfulfilled. It takes a whole soul to share a love that is whole in itself. When you are grounded in yourself, you can offer a love that is genuine and fulfilling. Snakes don't give birth to cats; neither does the moon twinkle.

The more your soul is convinced and reminded that it needs another to feel complete, the more it reinforces the belief that it is only half of what it could be. How unenlightened such a soul is when it perceives its source as limited, hence its half nature! Such a soul hoards any love it has within; such a soul is so creative in building dams and walls that it restricts its life flow and erects mental and emotional barriers.

Such a soul sees love as a means of getting rather than giving. Such a soul would rather die filled to the brim with gifts it has not shared than embrace the cold hands of death with a heart full of joy that comes from shared gifts and a soul as empty as space.

Why should love leave me empty? Your frightened heart may ask. If only it were imbued with the awareness that light can only fulfil its purpose as light if it chooses to embrace darkness.

Know today that your fear of fear is a guardian watching over a hidden treasure within you. You'll discover your true self in its maze when you tear down the thick walls erected within you by pain, conventional thinking, and repressed trauma and allow the light of love to guide you."

"What if I truly open up, expose my vulnerability, and love with all my heart, only for it to destroy me?" she asked the apostle.

"Yes, love can kill you; love will even tear you apart," the apostle acknowledged. Your deepest fear isn't death or being shattered; it's the painful realisation that a heart without cracks is a heart that cannot feel deeply. If death did not exist, your life would have no essence.

Woe to the soul that believes that death is its end. It digs the grave in which it will spend eternity. True happiness, which can last a long time, comes from a soul that understands that death is merely a doorway to Nirvana. In that state, God is everything, and everything is God, creating a New Earth where everything has meaning and yet is nothing.

A soul that allows fear to take control, surrounded by excuses, blame, and past traumas, will struggle to express and experience its true self. In its way, even a church rat can feel like a king in the reality it inhabits.

So, keep on loving, brethren. Love hard, love easy, and love freely; love until you are empty. Love until you have nothing more to give. To serve as a vessel, you must be willing to be emptied. A full vessel is of no use—just like a heart can't live if beating feels like a burden.

THE GAMUT AND SACRED ENIGMA OF LUST IN LOVE

You have said so much, Apostle, but my mind is slow to take in all that you have blessed our ears and watered our souls with. You've spoken of love with such delicate beauty, as if revealing hidden truths. Yet my heart lies encased beneath heavy stones—lifeless, silent, and buried deep. It yearns for something more than soft words; it needs something bold to crack open its tomb, let in the light, and feel the warmth of life once again..

My soul is troubled. I have my questions too, but I don't know if this is the right time to seek answers, Apostle?" Kwame asked.

A 38-year-old British-born Ghanaian, who bore his untamed impulses with a grin on his face, leaned forward slightly in a sitting position with his hands between his thighs.

His charming personality was without blemish, his laugh so infectious and elegantly attractive that it earned him a nickname among his fellow patients and the staff. His sympathetic smile belied the raging currents within him that caused his soul to react in ways he could not control.

The once-famous chef, who found comfort in the culinary arts, is now ruled by his appetite for sexual pleasures and quick thrills. His compulsive traits, exacerbated by his hypersexuality diagnosis, raged like an unstoppable torrent. The lustful temptations of substance abuse lured him further and further into the depths, where rage burst out of him like a blazing flame, devouring everything in its path.

He struggled with a rape conviction that irrevocably destroyed his identity and reputation and stamped his life with the tragic notes of disgrace. A once charming soul now found himself behind the confines of a psychiatric purgatory, where his broken spirit wandered amidst the shards of a life that was once exuberant, wild, and free.

“Surely you can, Kwame; every moment is always the right time to speak your heart. If life puts it in you, then be open enough to express yourself freely,” replied the apostle.

“The truth, dear Apostle, is that I often find myself wrestling with a dilemma. Are my moods and desires the turbulent storms that threaten to sink my ship, or are they the shining lighthouse that guides me safely through the currents of life?" He bowed his head slightly, unable to make eye contact with the apostle.

"As I traverse this long, shadowy road, paved with the burning residue of my struggles, I reflect on the true nature of my desires. Each step is marked by the weight of my OCD and the complexities of my hypersexuality, stirring a deep curiosity within me about what drives me forward. While the ominous threat of rape accusation spreads shadows within me, engulfing my thoughts and blinding me, it as become almost impossible to imagine breaking free from this internal bondage into the light of liberty.

Is my desire what traps my soul, or is it the key to rising above myself? Can I ever find peace while trying to hold onto something wild as I search for a calm place in life?" He asked, raising his head, both hands on his thighs, sitting upright, staring at the apostle, eagerly awaiting an answer.

"To the mind teeming with perversion, everything is perceived with a lustful gaze, my friend," replied the apostle.

"Is it not painfully clear – even to the blind, even in silence – that perversion, with endless hunger, sees your soul as its perfect match, longing to dance in dark harmony?"

Have you not also been taught by your prophets and teachers that whatever costume the spirit wears, the body performs as its character? Do you not realise that all life is a game and the thoughts are costumes to the mind?

But, apostle, I am besieged by these thoughts, and they poison my inner being. Kwame answered with an excruciating sigh. I am subject to their total authority."

"Aye, aren't the thoughts in your mind tightly woven by social norms and religious teachings?"

The apostle asked him in reply. "They portray the divine life forces as abominable and aberrant. They cast an opaque veil over the core of your existence. With the help of conventional thinking, they make it appear as absolute truth."

"So, what is the truth?

"What I have long regarded as truth has turned out to be the source of my despair, sorrow, and discontent," Kwame said, his gaze unwaveringly locked on the apostle, who scarcely blinked in response.

"You have been taught by your prophets and gurus, in all their holiness and divinity, to tame your desires. The public display of your enthusiasm and love of life is frowned upon by culture, as traders do with slaves.

Tradition wields sway over nations and moulds your desires into preconceived notions," the apostle said. "The masquerade your spirit wears, influencing the actions of your body, is crafted from the ideas and beliefs you have labelled as perversions. These are the deceptive illusions masquerading as truth, binding your spirit to a fate of eternal damnation."

The truth offered by others, shaped by dogmas and beliefs, is only temporary. You are the whole truth that your soul longs for. Manifesting means being fully aware of the space in existence where your desires fit into the bigger picture of life, rather than trying to numb it with ideas and tame it with dogmas and beliefs.

These misconceptions and ideas have thawed your soul and robbed it of all its divinity and charm, leaving swamps of frustration, rivers of guilt, and seas of unhappiness within to haunt you incessantly. The price of this confinement and suppression is a lack of expression in real life and a mountain of unfulfilled desires. They drain your energy as they remain in constant conflict, with your mind being the battlefield.

Sex, as energy, flows like a river, untamed and undisturbed, through all facets of daily life. Lust only causes the rippling of its surface; it is the wind that drives its flow. Any act of repression, non-acceptance, or denial of the divine self, essentially, the act of feeling, only hinders the flow of energy. This obstruction causes the energy within to continue to boil until it erupts like a volcano and burns away any awareness of self, love, compassion, and emotional intelligence.

What was created by the creative forces of time, space, and energy—an art and an act meant to inspire self-realisation, worship, adoration, and transcendence in this world—has instead become the root of all unconsciousness and the lonely path of self-destruction.

“But how can sex be an act of worship?” Kwame asked the apostle, startled. His brow furrowed slightly, and his eyes widened in surprise. His lips parted, forming a tentative and slightly uneven contour. “You speak in a way that is profound, but also confusing. Sex, as I have known it from childhood to this day, is a sin before God outside of marriage and therefore should only be practised within the auspices of marriage. At least that’s what I was taught, and I think you know that too. So, when you say sex is worship, I get confused. How can sin be seen as an act of worship?

Where in our journey through life are we not enlightened to the truth that our bodies are beautiful sanctuaries? Shouldn’t the place where the presence of God dwells be a sanctuary rather than a battlefield? Isn’t God worshipped, honoured, and revered in sanctuaries? Or is it not obvious that the woman, like the man, is the other self of God?

Sex in all its divinity, I tell you, is the door to all expressions of life, with orgasm as self-knowledge and the core of all enlightenment. Every act of moaning captures the bittersweet symphony of existence, a subtle cry of gratitude that dances on the edge of pleasure and pain, echoing like a haunting melody in the depths of the soul. All foreplays and romances are the intimacy of the soul with the whole of life in its entirety.

Why, then, did your ancestors and teachers demonise this intimate act of angels?

Sex, I say to you, is a pious dance of the universe. Like heavy chains binding the ankles of slaves, your gurus and sages have forged notions of impurity and hostility around sex, imprisoning you to the extent that the freedom it offers now dons the guise of perversion.

The perversion that gave rise to these ideas now serves as trauma in love events, sharing pain, and calling it pleasure. Have you not been told that God can also reveal Himself in all His glorious divinity during this eternal dance of the angels? Any attempt to drum the beats of pain during this dance numbs the God within, and when God is numbed, trauma is born.

So, how can nirvana be attained? I ask you, all ye whose souls walk the dark roads of desire. Do you revel in the storm? Have you forgotten that like terms must attract for a spark to exist? Why, then, have you transformed your wands into instruments of doom, crafting discordant melodies to disrupt the sacred dance of the gods?

Do you not know that the beats of both hearts on the dance floor of divine excitement must be in harmony for God to express and experience Himself?" The apostle asked, looking at the entire audience. As Kwame is, "so are we all," he said.

"So how do I find the balance so that the God in me can be expressed while experiencing the God in others; in love and divine vulnerability, during this dance you speak of?" Kwame inquired.

"Self-awareness, I exhort you, is the way. Self-awareness is the key that unlocks the treasures that lie in the presence and moments of all that God inhabits. With self-knowledge, you become the master of your river, steering its current amid the turbulent waves of desire.

You acknowledge your impulses without fear, expressing your wishes freely, yet you do so wrapped in love and total vulnerability. True strength emerges from this delicate balance of surrender and control.

But what is lust? You might ask. Lust weaves its fire into the eternal dance of angels, adding a vibrant spice to love's embrace. Love carries this passion with it, igniting every moment it touches, transforming the ordinary into the extraordinary. Without it, love loses its flavour as angels dance intimately, because love by itself is charming, holy, and flawless, but tasteless without lust, for lust is the fuel of attraction.

As you dance like angels, embrace your desires without fear, for in the act of longing, many find themselves utterly lost. And those who are afraid of losing themselves are terrified by the unrestrained dance of the angels. Give way to fear, and watch how it places your inner throne of grace on the threshold of perversion.

Only when you release the chains that confine your mind and recognise that sex is the sacred language of the universe, will you truly free your soul. In doing so, you'll uncover the profound beauty woven into the rhythms of life, flowing freely and endlessly. By breaking free from your limitations, you will awaken to your unique poetry of existence.

So, I urge you today, just as I did with your forebears: Journey boldly across the vast sea of human experience. Embrace your desires and the fervent passion that fuels them as powerful tools for forging deep connections with yourself and others. Let these intense emotions guide you in the sacred, intimate dance of angels.

THE LANGUAGE OF THE HOLY ECHOES

"Er, sorry o," the Nigerian member of staff called from the back of the hallway near the door where she sat with other staff and nurses. "Sorry to interrupt you, but if I let this question go unspoken now, I might forget it," she said with an embarrassed smile. "Sorry, Apostle, I don't know if this question differs from what the others have asked, but I still need clarification," she said.

"There is no wrong or right question, my dear," the apostle replied calmly.

“All right then!” She exclaimed, followed by a sigh of relief as she spoke. The thing is, I am a devout Christian, and I believe in our Lord and Saviour, Jesus Christ. I want to know what the purpose of prayer is. Why do we pray? Is it that God does not hear us and that he wants us to remind him of our needs every morning? Isn’t it a waste of time to pray if God already knows our thoughts before we say them? Or is praying just a mental cardio for a hopeless spirit?

Her voice rained down like raindrops on rooftops as she aired out her inner frustration in the form of questions.

I earnestly long to reach the heart of God, Apostle. Some say that prayer moves mountains, but I do not want to move mountains; I want to move God. So is the essence of prayer praise, because it is also said that praise moves God? Or is praise the right act of prayer? Please, teach me to pray properly, if there is such a thing. My soul longs to pray properly; I want to touch the heart of God when I am absorbed in that moment of prayer. I want my tears to reach God’s ears and my words to fill his heart. I want my knees to be firmly anchored in his presence and before his throne of grace,” she pleaded.

The apostle paused and grinned. “But you just prayed right,” he said. A feeling of doubt and despair spread across the Nigerian lady’s face. “But how can that be?” she asked with widened eyes and raised eyebrows. “I was just trying to ask the question that I have always had buried inside me: how is that prayer?” she asked, confused.

“Prayer is the mother tongue of divine beings,” replied the apostle. It is the greatest mode of communicating with the God within and with all who share realms with the self.

I still don’t understand what you mean,” she said to the apostle in reply. “Can you explain better what you mean when you say, “Share realms with self?”

“Is the self, not God, and God, all that the self is?” the apostle asked her. “How deeply have you immersed yourself in being human that you’ve forgotten the powerful truth of your existence as a being?”

Are you not called a human being? Does that not mean a human God or God having a human experience?

Stagnant water has lingered so long in its stillness that it thinks of itself as a serene pond. It yearns for rain to swell and expand, forgetting that the very rain it prays for is not separate from its essence. In its desire for growth, it overlooks the truth: it is already connected to the storm it seeks. The soul has longed for the presence of God so that it can be powered to express itself and experience itself, but is also blind to the awareness that to be itself is to be God.

How can you know or experience God if you are afraid to experience being human? Or have you not been taught or conditioned to know that man, like every other vessel that possesses life, is the other self of God, that is, its reflection?

Why does a beggar handle pans incessantly? He goes home with full pots, but his chest of needs is eternally empty. Every dawn brings with it the promise of new goals—a chance to wield pans with creativity and courage. Why do you fight, Man-God? Why do you take up arms against the woman-god? How perplexing it is that in the moments when you could allow the divine within you to shine, you instead wore the mask of mere humanity. Yet, in times when you should embrace your human experience, you find yourself trying to embody a role far beyond your reach, as if you were playing God. It's a dance of contradictions that leaves us questioning where our true selves reside.

Were you not taught years ago by the wisest of all man-gods? Did he not teach you that there is a time for everything and every event under the sun? Did he not tell your fathers that there is a time to give birth to God and that there is a time to let God die so that it can be born again? Were you not listening?

Prayer has evolved into a mental exercise that stirs your desires and entices your mind to craft convincing thoughts from pain, thoughts that ignite the candle of hope to give your mind a sense of purpose.

The pain that comes with being human contains within it the core of being, a sign of life, and the inner desire to be. Yet one casts, binds, and runs away from this very pain, asking the God that the mind has created to help save the day and banish every pain and challenge.

But we overlook a truth: even the God our minds have crafted draws its essence from the vibrant energy that fuels existence. This God, driven by false desires, becomes like a panhandler, always seeking what it lacks.

How and where would the transition from man to God and from God to man take place if not in darkness, embraced by total acceptance and unwavering love? How could a new day be born if the sun did not accept its intimacy with the pain that the dark sky serves?

Yet only the man-god handles pans and asks himself to suppress that which is his purpose of being—to experience and express all of life in divine totality.

Moreover, if God wanted to be fully God, it would just rest in pure beingness. Even in that state, devoid of thought or the mind, there would be no experience or awareness to remind it of its own identity.

Having thoughts that drift like the clouds in the sky and ebb like great and ancient seas within the mind is a testament to our humanity. These thoughts give meaning to man's self-expression and experience of God.

What should remind you of yourself in the presence of lack now pulls you to a path of amnesia, making you crave things that appear to represent the self. In this pursuit, you seek to find what the self can provide for itself, yet, in doing so, you lose sight of your true self while desperately and endlessly searching for it.

You, the mighty architects of existence, have ensnared the divine, locking it away with the chains of ignorance. You bind its hands with burdensome words, weigh down its legs with the chill of uncried tears, and drown out its voice with the cacophony of sorrowful wails. You stake its essence upon an altar of sacrifices, rendering its strength feeble through battles fought without meaning. Meanwhile, you blindfold its vision with scraps of fabric, stitched from the fabric of names, titles, and labels that it never chose to wear."

In the face of adversity, you have made God weak. In the face of health, you made God sick. In the face of lack, you have mated God with a church mouse, and in the face of love, God lies helpless, oppressed, and devoured by fear.

You implore solutions in distant heavens curated by the mind, in well-articulated and verbalised verbs and nouns.

In distant worlds filled with utopian realities, pain and suffering seem to have no place, yet we often forget that the divine is at the heart of who we are. It comes alive not only in joy and happiness but also in our struggles and challenges.

For what use is God if there is nothing to create? How can God creatively save the day if there is no challenge to face? You have ruthlessly stripped away its very essence, dismissing its profound presence within you in blind pursuit of conventional ideas and beliefs.

How much does the farmer who plants trees weep, begging to reap fruit from the same tree whose planting he has not endured? The farmer is aware that the greatest prayer he has to do is to endure the pain of tilling the soil and planting a crop.

He is merely a vessel, through which life itself, the true farmer, harnesses the profound forces of time and space to transmute the seeds buried in anguish into a magnificent, blossoming tree of hope.

How foolish and useless it is for a farmer to ignore the hard work of preparing the soil and planting the seeds, hoping instead that God will miraculously take over and do it all for him. The farmer must use the strength and life given to him to do the work himself if he wants to enjoy the harvest. The prodigal son, I beseech you, is more righteous than such a farmer.

Truly, the sense marked "common" does not grow in everyone's garden; ironically, everyone possesses its seed.

If only the farmer recognised that he is merely a vessel waiting to be filled by life, he might understand that praying for a harvest from a tree he has yet to plant is futile. Such prayers should be seen as a dialogue with the divine, reminding him of his true nature and the connection between humanity and God.

They serve as a reminder that when he plants, God is planting alongside him, for he is filled with divine potential. Instead of using prayer to plead with God, he should embrace his role as a steward of creation, remembering that he is meant to govern the earth, not beg for what he has the power to cultivate himself.

But the farmer has become so addicted to words that he thinks they create the melody to which God, life, or the universal mind dances to. His soul is numb to the profound truth that words are a potent force, a fiery energy that compels him to break the earth and sow the seeds of his desires. This energy is nothing less than God in motion, urging him to take action and shape his destiny.

The Nigerian female member of staff listened intently, as did the rest of the audience, without saying a word while the apostle continued to speak.

Were you not listening when your preachers and gurus taught you about words? Is the word not God, and God the word? Is the word not a seed of thought? Are thoughts not the fruit of experiences? Are seeds not found in the fruit of experiences? Are the fruits not found hanging on different branches of the tree of life? Isn't each branch a representation of different life experiences and expressions in its divine totality? Is the tree of life not rooted in the sands of time but powered and grounded in love and ego? Are love and ego not the different faces of God? Are you not the tree of life? Are you, not God, creatively playing man and woman, masculine and feminine, positive and negative, wearing the costume of humanness, expressing and experiencing self as human and through human?

Truly, I tell you, as I have warned your ancestors, your teachers, and those who boldly claim to be the faithful. It is utterly foolish to shy away from challenges while yearning for miracles. You will be like a farmer who fervently prays for an abundant harvest but cowardly flees from the backbreaking toil of tilling the soil and planting the seeds.

What would a good day be without victories won? Are victories not a memento of battles fought? No wonder your prayers are ceaseless and never-ending; you seek medals of victory in battles you refused to fight. Have you not been reminded that the backbone of prayer is self-belief, and the blood that flows through its veins is hard work?

For what is prayer without work and the Spirit of God but an empty echo—impotent, lifeless, and still as the dead sea?

Aye, be constructive in thy use of words and when you creatively work. For God is drained of energy when words are used in vain and when work is done on things that are wanted but not needed.

Don't be like those who rely on others for words and hope, believing they lack the right tools to overcome obstacles and clear the thorns on the path to personal transformation.

Everyone has the right words to speak and the right tools to use. Grace, powered by belief in oneself, guides each person to use their gifts in their own way.

But if you want to be guided by your will as to how your own words should be structured, strive to make your words creative and just so that they serve as alarm clocks and tools for labour, not pans for panhandling. When it comes to praise, don't forget to see it for what it essentially is: words in rhythm.

Let your words be a catalyst for awakening, a gentle reminder of the vessel each person is and the divine spark within that fuels their journey. Recognise that every action taken and every challenge embraced is a sacred act—a divine dance that invites God to work through us. In this continuous act of planting, we engage in the profound art of self-expression, nurturing not only our growth but also the beauty of existence itself.

"In all my life, I have never heard words as fulfilling as what you said, Apostle," the Nigerian woman said in shock. "Now I feel like I have been wasting my time all these years praying for the same things I have, but convinced that I lack. This clearly shows that I have been stressing myself out and looking for something to hope for instead of creating something. I never knew that the greatest act of hope is creation.

I have seen every challenge as a means to cry out to God instead of opening myself up so the God within me can express itself through me to meet the challenge, she lamented dejectedly.

The problem is not that I lack faith, which is why my miracle didn't happen. The truth is that I lack faith in myself and knowledge of who I am. I also have not chosen to take responsibility and fight my battles in love and with love, knowing that it is not me but the God within me that does all through me.

"Weep not, for even God needs a moment of repose. And in ignorance, God has His best nap," the apostle replied.

"The whole essence of prayer is to awaken God, but if it is not awakened within you while you pray, then in vain will your prayers be."

WARLORDS, MARTYRS, AND PEACEMAKERS

"So, tell me, what would you say about better days? What would you say about peace? It's so easy to say all this, but you and I know things don't work that way, Mr. Apostle."

"Prayer is work. How beautiful that sounds to my ears, Oh, hallelujah!" The amputee soldier from the Democratic Republic of Congo said mockingly, disguising his voice and rocking back and forth angrily in his wheelchair as he exclaimed. "Maybe the God in me was not woke enough to answer my prayer by not turning what I prayed for into reality.

Or maybe I didn't pray right, huh? Well, I am not fucking religious, but damn, I have been working; I even worked my fucking legs off. Isn't that a prayer, too, according to you? I did my job; I was great at it. For peace, I pulled every trigger, and for better days, I slashed every skin. For what I believed in, I raised my country's flag; for love, I sang her war songs. You have seen wars, haven't you?

Well, I have fought for ideas, for noble and selfish ideals, for beliefs and faith, for things I knew nothing about, and for orders I had to obey, in all regions of Africa and on battlefields far beyond.

And what did I get for the prayers answered due to the work I did, for the wars I fought, and for the peace I won but never experienced or lived? I got a title of national hero, a martyr's medal, a military star, two lost legs, ego-boosting words, manic depression, and PTSD," the war veteran lamented.

"Is war not supposed to bring peace? The war is won, but peace is what I never found. Rather, the ghosts of the eerie memories I gained as trophies are constantly haunting me," he bewailed as he slowly stopped rocking his wheelchair, lowered his head, covered his face with the palm of his right hand, propped his elbows on his thighs, and sobbed quietly.

The atmosphere became chilly and silent; no one had seen the war veteran in such a sober and sombre mood since his admission. All they knew were his constant aggressive outbursts, his self-blame, and the self-harming act of deliberately falling out of his wheelchair to attract attention.

The apostle sat up, walked towards him, sat down on an empty chair next to his wheelchair, facing the rest of the audience, and began to speak.

"Wars, my friends, are monstrous tempests that ravage fertile fields into wastelands and transform bustling cities into ghost towns. They shatter bodies like fragile pottery and cloud minds with the darkness of despair. In their wake, they leave humanity smoldering in ashes, echoes of dreams silenced by a cataclysmic roar."

The peace that is sought in the loins of war—how deadly and detrimental, will such peace be?

Its heart would only dance to the beat of fear. Illusory expectations and oppressive conditions will shape its bones and cartilage. Its veins and arteries will be made of servitude and insecurity, driven by external dependence.

Aye, how deeply does love flow through their veins? Their very essence and existence are bound to an unwavering resolve to judge, paired with a relentless yearning to gather, possess, and exert control over all they encounter. How war-thirsty and battle-hungry such a peace will become! Indeed, oaks do not bear sycamore fruit, and no war like the oak tree would bear peace like sycamore fruit.

Truly, only peace can give birth to peace; for war will certainly and undoubtedly give birth to war. Even if its skin, face, and body are coloured and shaped to resemble peace, its being and soul will still be war."

The apostle paused, took a deep breath, leaned forward, turned his head, looked at the veteran, and said almost conspiratorially, "So fallen is your soul; how deeply have you dragged God over the coals burnt by your ego-driven mind? You have berated its throne, and now a slave you have become, spending every moment of your miserable existence earnestly struggling and fighting to gain what you already possess."

Who made thee warlord, O ye Man-God? Existence, the world so old and blue, the divinely orchestrated and creatively sculpted universal theatre of dreams, thy mighty hands and manly minds have turned to an eternal colosseum. God now lives its life within you, fighting battles it knows nothing about, for an illusory sense of peace your ego promises that your soul never experiences.

Fighting hast thou made a sign of life for God. For peace, you fight wars. For love, you fight hate. For light, you fight darkness, and for strength, you fight weakness. For riches, you fight poverty; for abundance, you fight scarcity. But in all thy fighting, peace lies in isolation, suffocated, drained of purpose, covered by the veil of false beliefs, tied up with ropes of ego-stricken ideas, and left for dead.

For titles, ye have ordained thyself warlords. To be called martyrs and heroes, you have fought good fights of faith and fate with love and light as thy flag.

For the love you have for the land, you waged wars to bring peace to the land. Out of love for its government, ye have patriotically pledged yourselves to live by its noble ideals and to preserve them. And to keep those ideals alive, ye have ended lives.

To be called national heroes, ye have thrived diligently in all these wars. How divine your ego must be! Oh, Oh ye warlords! Your wars, ye have transcended, shifting from the physical realm to the battlegrounds of the mind. The title you once won and wore around your neck is now an adornment of ego-driven feelings, emotions, self-esteem, and identities."

The apostle stood up in a trice. Turning to the audience, he stared and asked loudly, "Are your minds not carrying out the will of thy land? Are you not its government? Is your body not the highly adored executive arm of your land, carrying out the will of that inner dominion? Is your level of emotional intelligence not as that of the legislative arm, crafting the laws by which you live, and your soul–the silent judge–the judicial arm of your land?

Verily, I say to you, woe unto the soul that wages war to find peace. Peace can only be sought by being peaceful. Such a soul will call gloom and dejection friends. It seeks love by going to war with hatred, for love can only be obtained through loving.

In the lake of unhappiness and misery, such a soul will constantly swim. It battles against darkness in a quest to uncover the light, for light is not merely the absence of darkness, but rather a brighter hue of it. True light can only be discovered by shining forth. The soul is light, and when light shines in darkness, it embraces darkness and instantly becomes one with it, not by trying to fight and conquer it.

Does the sun fight with the night sky in search of daylight? Behold, the sun becomes intimate with the night sky, disguised as the moon. Its light shines so brightly that the dark sky melts into it, and thus daylight is born.

So much have your seers and gurus told you that life is hard, so you fight with life to conquer its hardness and possess it. Endless alarms have been sounded by the guardians of your reality, from the day you were born until the day you inhale, never to exhale, that you are, only when you own things. Whatever spoils thy hands touches as you war to own, guard them with your life and never let them go, for they are what make you human and alive. How sad such a tale is, and how humiliating such advice!

Verily, life is hard for souls who perceive life as work. To such souls, life is a war, and as a diligent warlord, fighting is their soul's purpose.

When you work, you expect a wage, just as in war you expect spoils, so you put your all into all the battles you wage, every moment of your existence on the battlefield of the mind and in the eternal colosseum you call reality. Diligently do you work, and with hard work do you fight, earnestly expecting a wage from existence. Life indeed should be hard for you, for only fools would create wars to impress life. Everything is life, and that which you war with is also a second self of life.

Would I go to war with myself just to gain ownership? Isn't it deeply contradictory to inflict pain on your soul? Is everything that has life, not life itself? Why then do you war against yourself? Why create battles and make life moments a survival series for the sake of illusory ideas, words, dogmas, selfish desires, power, fate, faith, lands, titles, and medals?

Oh, ye Man-Gods turned warlords, the apostle called, staring at the audience. Woe unto thee for the souls you have laid to rest, for the self-esteems you mercilessly stabbed and left to bleed in the wake of your cunning war. Your betrayal echoes through the shadows, a haunting reminder of the lives you've shattered in your ruthless pursuit.

How proficient you are with your arms of mass destruction, and for all you have destroyed! To your waning soul, every warlord emerges as a thief and a foe, a spectre of betrayal that seeks to seize your essence. Hence, you erect walls as lofty as the ancient giants of the forest, guarding what you cherish yet do not truly possess from one another. In your fervour, you forget that the true thief is time itself. When the moment arrives, all that you love and have fought so hard to keep will be quietly taken from you, for ultimately, all belongs to life itself.

Yet, if the warlord can lay down his arms, renounce his badge, and raise the white flag of peace, I tell you, he will become a true peacemaker. With the profound understanding that life is intertwined with self, and self is but a reflection of life, he will embrace a transformative experience that elevates the peacemaker to greatness. Fighting with life when it expresses itself through its vessels is fighting with oneself. For self can't war its reflection, neither can substance war its shadow.

Peace, I believe, can only be achieved by embracing a peaceful mindset. A true peacemaker embodies tranquillity; their presence radiates calmness. They recognise that we possess nothing of true value, so why should they engage in battles over things that cannot be owned—be it ideas, rules, emotions, land, or even life itself? Understanding this, they cultivate serenity within themselves, allowing peace to blossom both in their hearts and in the world around them. Peacemakers are those who are at peace with life, so every moment of existence is a moment of peaceful expression, of total oneness, and of acceptance of what is. They know that eternity is a lie and every moment is the truth.

So, be ye peacemakers. Make peace with thyself if ye truly desire to be peaceful.

For in war, life is not lived, but in peace, rest is assured. Even God, in all of its magnanimity, lives when it rests, for in peace is peace attained, and when peace is attained, rest is thus found."

The words of the apostle penetrated the veteran's soul, releasing emotions that had been buried for a very long time. As he felt the guilt of years of conflict lifted from his shoulders, tears began to trickle down his aged cheeks. He felt an overwhelming sense of inner serenity encircling his spirit for the very first time, while everyone watched soberly in silence.

THE ULTIMATE EUCHARIST

“As the psychotherapeutic event drew to a close, the moderating occupational therapist took the stage. Her eyes reflected the journey of each individual who had shared their vulnerabilities, silent struggles, inner wars, and torments.

“As the sun’s light begins to wane, I would like to express my heartfelt gratitude to everyone gathered here today,” she said softly. “Those who were vulnerable enough to share whatever their hearts allowed them, those who were open enough to receive and learn from the experiences of others, those who were shy to speak, pointing to the staff at the back of the room, I hope you find the courage to speak next time,” she said with a mischievous smile on her face.

The nurses at the back of the hall laughed out loud. “Well, she’s talking to you; I hope you are aware of that.” Dr. Ade asked the nurse next to him sarcastically. “I know, right?” replied the nurse. “Maybe next time I will have the courage to do the same as the others. But how am I supposed to say out loud that my marriage is not working or that I am tired of raising my child alone?

As an African woman, I can’t wash my dirty pants in public. Besides, how do you want them to perceive me after the event?

Well, I think I understand what you are getting at, but it’s all right,” replied Dr. Ade.

“I want to take this opportunity to thank Dr. Ade, who organised this great event, and the management, who ensured that this event was a success. Apostle, I cannot thank you enough; we are all grateful for your insightful words.”

The patients and staff in the room erupted in applause and cheers, all but one— the Sudanese psychiatrist, who had recently been assigned to the facility alongside Dr Ade. He lingered in the shadows of the crowded function room, his steely demeanour and sharp mind at work as he quietly observed the apostle’s interactions with other residents. With keen attention, he documented the apostle’s events and profound insights, which posed a potential threat to the sinister agenda of the hospital’s management.

While everyone rejoiced, the apostle stood there in amazement, didn’t say a word, just smiled, and sat down again.

"I hope we get a cigarette reward after tea," the veteran called out to the nurse." Again, the hall burst into laughter. "We will see how that goes," the OT replied with a smile.

"So yeah, the management has said that this event will happen often to promote group cohesion and healing, "she continued. On behalf of the management, the staff, and everyone who has contributed in one way or another to the success of today, I say a heartfelt thank you for all your patience and your audience."

"Dr. Ade, you could take over the moderation for the next edition," the nurse said with a laugh. "Or maybe the staff will put up someone of their choice because this edition was championed by the residents represented by the apostle."

"Thank you again, Apostle! This event was truly life-changing. Let us draw the curtain so we can all have our tea and a few cigarettes for those who smoke."

The atmosphere erupted again in laughter at the OT's statement. The patients made their way to their respective wards and rooms. Some of the staff made their way to the garden to smoke a cigarette, while some went to the staff office.

Just as the apostle made his way to the pharmacy to ask for some medication, Dr. Ade hurried after him. However, the African nurse, who had been standing silent next to him throughout the event, had discreetly approached the apostle first, unbeknownst to him.

“How could you know all that you said during the event?” she asked the apostle.

“They were just schizophrenic rants,” the apostle replied, with a huge grin on his face. “Now you are taking a piss,” she replied morosely.

“Why are you sad? Did any of the rants make sense to you?” the apostle asked.

“Not only did it make sense, it also sparked something within me, bringing to light much of what I had deliberately suppressed for a long time,” she replied.

“Truth is, I am gradually losing life as I strive to live,” she replied. “I do not know what is happening to me. Raising my child alone, in the shadow of neglect by his absent father, has darkened the core of who I once was. I stare in the mirror and do not recognise the woman I see.”

“Well, I was not brave enough to raise my hands and speak my mind as others dared to do during the event. But then, I am sad because this should have been a once-in-a-lifetime opportunity. Now the event is over, and my heart is still troubled because I am struggling with questions that I should have asked but did not, because I was so worried about what people would say,” she lamented angrily.

“That shouldn’t make you sad, my dear; you don’t need an event to express your feelings. I am still locked up in this madhouse,” said the apostle, laughing softly, “so we can talk about anything.”

"Hey Apostle, I'd like to talk to you," Dr. Ade called from behind as they approached the dispensary. "We can talk after tea, Doc," the apostle replied. "I belong to Her Royal Highness; can't you see that?" The apostle asked, pointing at the nurse. "Yes, I can see just fine," replied Dr. Ade with a smile on his face.

"But if the word you want to say is brief, we can just sit in the lounge while she gets me the medication I asked for," the apostle said to Dr Ade, who replied with a nod in total agreement.

"Has anyone told you anything about your forthcoming tribunal?" Dr. Ade asked the apostle as they entered the lounge. "I mean one of the nurses who was on duty this week," he prompted.

"I have not. No one has ever said anything about it, but I love it here. There have been no incidents lately, so I feel like I am settling in perfectly and making new friends, too. I have been here for over four weeks, have I not?" asked the apostle.

"Yes, in two days it will be exactly 4 weeks and 4 days, so I am not surprised that you already love it here. I think you will make even more friends after our amazing experience today. Though there's something you are not telling me, and I think if you do, it will help in solidifying my plea," Dr Ade replied.

"What plea are you talking about?" The apostle asked with a scrunched nose and furrowed brow. "The reason I wanted to talk to you is that I'm going on holiday in four days, which will be right after your tribunal. Since you haven't had any serious episodes since your last visit and your relationships with everyone on the ward are going well, they're considering moving you to a place closer to home. The only thing is, I don't even know where that is.

Honestly, it makes no sense to me that someone who spoke in words my ears have never heard before cannot remember his name or where he lives, no identity whatsoever. Who are you really, apostle? What is your name? Where do you live? I need all these pieces of information to ensure we get you a suitable and comfortable place to live. Otherwise, the council will step in, and you know what that means: they will find a place that doesn't suit your preferences. Besides, winter is coming, and considering your age and current health condition, you mustn't find yourself in an unsuitable environment or sleeping outside in the cold."

"You must try to remember so that I can help you. I want to help you, Apostle."

"Why are you so eager to help? What is different from here and everywhere?" asked the apostle gruffly. "I didn't mean to upset you," Dr. Ade replied, noticing the slightly raised tone in the apostle's voice.

"Haunted by fractured realities," the apostle thus vented. "I am not upset; I am only disappointed. How dearly you all claim to care, while in the end, you have reasons for your actions. I understand you want to help; that sounds empathic, but I wouldn't buy it."

"I didn't mean to upset you, apostle. I just felt that you deserved more. And yes, it will make me happy. If that means I am being selfish and doing this for my gain, then so be it. If this is how I can repay you for giving me the torch I needed to return to myself, then I will gladly do it.

You know what? I now believe in all that you said, that life is a thing of divine arrangement and not chance, because I believe that my assignment to come to this ward for a few weeks was all I needed. I was going crazy, and my relationship with myself and others was breaking down, but hearing you speak gave me the courage I needed to know that I wasn't the only one who was crazy."

The apostle was startled, stared, and did not say a word.

"Listen, I do not want to patronise you and force you to tell me anything. I know you might think I am saying this to make you change your mind and give me the information I need," Dr. Ade pleaded. "But that's not the case; even if you don't, I just want to do what makes my soul feel alive. And that's making sure you are properly sorted when you leave here. I shouldn't tell you this, but I have just found out that they want to get rid of you quickly because your presence here is a problem for the new management. They think you will make disciples of yourself here, and they don't want that."

"I think they heard you talking and thought that everything you said was full of delusions and grandiose speeches.

Moreover, given that others here are struggling as well, they are likely to believe that everything you say is true.

I don't blame them; they don't understand. But yes, the mind cannot experience or express life beyond its level of consciousness. I am just saying that even if you leave, I want to make sure you're in a safe place. And to do that, I need the details I asked for," Dr. Ade said.

"Your superiors wear friendly masks in this madhouse, but false intentions resonate in their hearts," the apostle replied. "They speak of compassion and understanding, but every decision seems like a stitch in the coat of pleasure and greed that their intentions wear.

Their empathy is just a show for the onlookers who believe we are damaged. In their scenic illusion, which they call reality, we are clowns, and the ringmasters pretend to be concerned while they tighten the ropes of our suffering, because our suffering is their pleasure. Even as we take pills to serve as antidotes, calming our minds and silencing the voices within, the turmoil of discontent and ennui continues to swell.

The healers are often the primary source of inner discomfort for those yearning for healing, and we, the so-called abnormal souls, find ourselves mourning this paradoxical reality created by those who shape existence. In this realm, life serves as both refuge and an infirmary for the soul.

I appreciate your kind gestures, to be honest, but you owe me nothing. What I have shared with you is only my experience, and my path is different, just as your path is different. My words, even if they are labelled delusional because of my condition, can only serve as a light to help you illuminate yours even as you create your own experience.

Are you in debt to the sun? Does it not serve you much greater light than any words anyone can share or any love anyone can express? Have you paid the debt you claim to owe nature for the light it serves you?

I was here before you, and I will still be here long after you have gone, so why worry about me? Think of yourself first, because you need much more care, healing, a home, and a mind full of peace than you think someone else does. Your intentions are pure; needless to say, let them guide you in all your actions.

"Those whose hearts are filled with light will embrace your actions with the same warmth with which they were offered. So once more, let your intentions be pure and brimming with light," the apostle said.

Doctor Ade, basking in the truth that filled the atmosphere, remained silent. "It was a moment of communion with the eternal truth beyond clinical labels.

I am but a tiny piece in the patchwork of life, Doctor, a citizen of its colossal fabric," the apostle said as she stepped closer to Dr. Ade.

"Abdul Malik, a name boldly carved into the primordial winds of the universe, is the only detail I can share," the apostle whispered. "Is that the only thing you can remember? Who were you before the mists of this state? That's all I am asking—where did you live?" confused yet enthralled, Dr. Ade inquired.

The apostle grinned, an eclectic mix of shattered memories. "The thing is, we run the risk of losing the essence of the present if we chase after the enigmatic ghosts of the mediaeval past. I am a nomad in this space, constantly travelling, flowing, evolving, expressing, and experiencing new facets of myself.

Abdul Malik is only a tiny part of the big picture, but his presence is as important as the breath itself. I am but a humble entertainer moving in the realms of fact and fantasy in this brief dance called existence. I live in the hearts of those who fearlessly and unapologetically search for themselves.

'The chosen ones, the exceptional souls who sail fearlessly and lovingly across the ancient sea of life, gently row their boats as they untangle the intricate dream of existence."

"So, if you want to know where I lived," the apostle urged, "then search your soul. If you are interested in making a place for me when I leave this place, then make room for my words in your heart, because my words are a part of me."

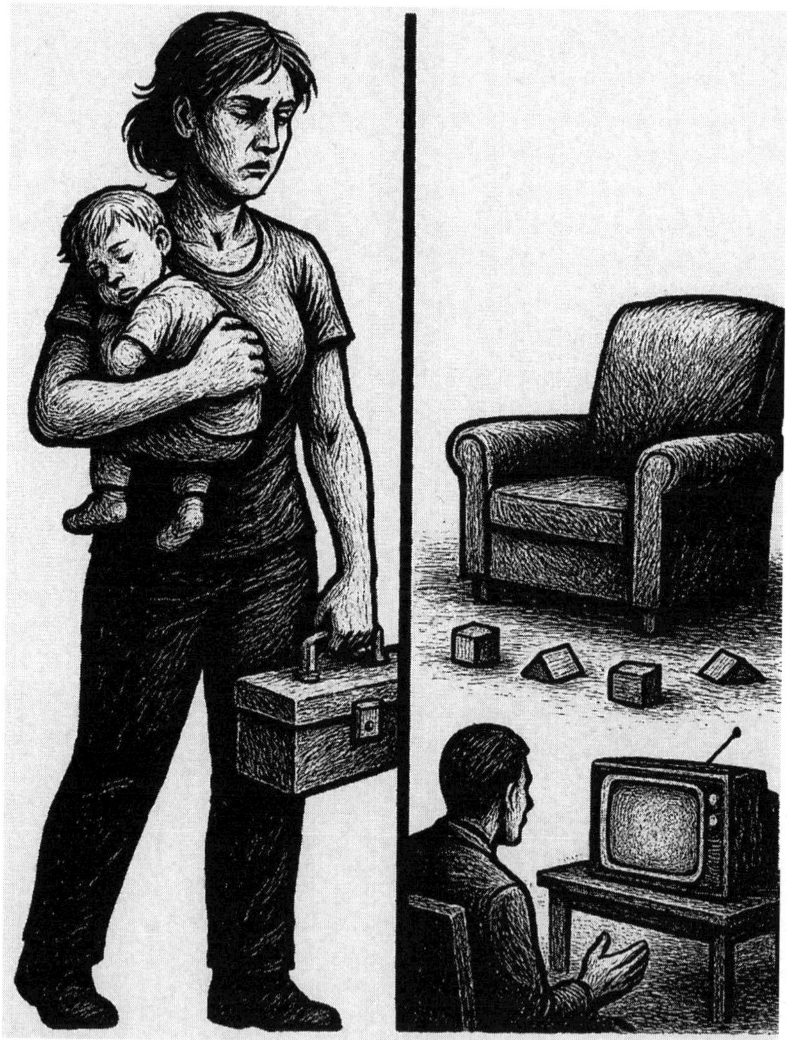

MASCULINE MUMS & DEADBEAT DADS

Just as Dr. Ade was about to answer the apostle, "The nurse walked into the lounge with the medication the apostle requested. Forgive me for interrupting your conversation," she said, staring at the two of them. "Doctor, can you help me hold the medication so I can get the apostle a cup of water to take it with?"

The nurse asked, handing Dr. Ade the cup with the medication. "Do not worry, my dear," Dr. Ade replied, taking the medicine cup from her. "This doesn't seem to be the PRN I requested for Your Highness?" The apostle asked, staring at the medicine cup as he handed it to Dr. Ade. "No, Apostle," replied the nurse.

"This is risperidone. It's already time for your evening medication, you know, and you just had a PRN two hours ago."

"All right, I could swallow it while I wait for the cup of water," the apostle insisted. "Yes, I know you can, Apostle," she replied coolly. "But it will be better to swallow it with water, so wait a moment.

I will go to the dining room and get you a cup of water. As you wish, Your Highness," replied the apostle with a broad grin on his face.

"What about your relationship? How are things going now? You mentioned that earlier with a sad face," The apostle asked Dr. Ade, just as the nurse walked into the dining room. Dr. Ade took a deep breath and slowly wiped his mouth with the palm of his left hand as he exhaled slowly.

"You don't have to speak if you don't feel like it," the apostle emphasised. "I just feel like I've heard you say something like that. But maybe that's just the thoughts in my head. I think I need to take my medication now," the apostle said and chuckled.

"Here we are," called the nurse as she entered the lounge. Dr. Ade handed the medicine to the apostle. He took the cup with his right hand, emptied it into his left palm, tilted his head back, and gently placed the medicine on his tongue. He took the cup of water handed to him by the nurse and drank it down. "Thank you," the apostle said gratefully and handed the cups back to the nurse, who squeezed the medicine cup and threw it into the trash can next to the door she was standing in front of, and handed the empty cup of water to the member of staff passing by the entrance to the lounge.

"What time is it on your wristwatch? I left my watch on the desk in the office," she asked Dr. Ade. "You can note half past six as the time the medication was taken," Dr. Ade replied, staring at his wristwatch. She brought out the pod from her pocket, updated the time the medication was taken, and dipped the pod back into her pocket.

"So, are we still going to have that brief conversation we were going to have before Dr. Ade snatched you away from me?" She asked the apostle shyly. "No, he didn't snatch me away from you," scoffed the apostle.

"Your Highness, you can come and get him back," Dr. Ade replied, grinning at the nurse. "Well, Dr. Ade is my brother, so he can stay while we talk. I have had this conversation with him before, and I don't want to miss this golden opportunity again. But you seem to have had a good time; I hope you don't mind, Doc?" "Do not worry, my dear, I don't mind," replied Dr. Ade.

"Your meal will be ready in an hour. That's enough time for me to finally bear my mind," the nurse said to the apostle as she walked up to him and sat down in the empty seat next to him.

It still amazes me that the one who needs our guidance is now the one from whom we seek guidance. Abdul Malik's name alone sounds Islamic, but he says he doesn't believe in religion. This old man is the most mysterious schizophrenic patient I have ever met. But his words are light. I cannot deny that, but still, Dr. Ade thought to himself and stared at the apostle while the nurse sat down next to him.

"All I was just trying to say earlier is that I am tired, apostle," the nurse bemoaned. "Is it a crime for one to desire to be understood? Is it so much for a woman to crave to be cared for and to be loved even by her kid, who now despises her because she barely spends time with him, even though I am toiling to give him the best life he can have as a child? I barely have a life, apostle.

However, despite my suffering, I am forced to continue being the rock of love, building resilience out of the shattered promises his good-for-nothing dad gave me in the form of love and hope. I am resolute in my determination to be both the mother and father because that is the only way I can navigate the capsized ship life has forced me to stare alone in this turbulent sea of single parenthood.

Like sand slipping through my fingertips, I can feel the remnants of my femininity vanishing. It is painful because I can't do anything about it but to simply watch all that makes me feel like a woman being ripped off of me forcefully by unfavourable life circumstances. All I have to face are financial difficulties and emotional obligations.

The nurse's pupils dilated as her hands tightened into fists. "I'm not sure how to go about rectifying this. How can I convey my immense affection for my son? How can I be the woman I used to be again? I'm sick of being the strong person all the time. But who is going to support us if I soften and let go?" Is my soul averse to love and affection? Or is love not designed for strong black women like me who have ambitions, plans, goals, and desires to be seen, loved, and adored?" she lamented.

"Well, the system has long been unfavourable to black women, so I am not surprised. What do we have to gain by trying to do better than these male folks who only know how to bend women over but do not care about their shit when it spills?" she fumed in a slightly raised tone. "I am sorry, Apostle and Doc; you are all good men, but that doesn't change my opinion of men, because they are part of the problem. "The unfortunate person life brought to me is nothing more than an idiot who messed himself up, believing that I was the one he hurt and abandoned."

The apostle listened intently, his gaze fixed on her, while Dr. Ade remained silently attentive, absorbing her words as she continued to lament.

"Men have no place in the fight for equality. I am not surprised, for the oppressor can never offer you the freedom to be his equal or the space to express yourself. My child has heeded his father's counsel. All my attempts to be a good mother and to play the role of father have been in vain. He believes that I drove Dad out of his life when all Mum wanted was to be loved and accepted."

"But you must not generalise, my dear. Not all men are like that, and it would be insensitive to think that all men are like that because of one unfortunate experience with a man," Dr. Ade said, interrupting her wailing. “Sometimes men have good intentions as well, but these women are taught to challenge and question our masculinity, which leads them to deny their womanhood in a quest for equality with men.

Haven’t you heard that there can’t be two captains on one ship?” he asked her. “Men are often seen as the culprits; however, many women today seek to take charge because they have been conditioned to believe that this is the only way to be recognised and valued. They scream that they want love and care, but how can you want love and care when your heart doesn’t even accept or know what love and care are?

In all sincerity, I get angry when I talk about this because I am tired of ungrateful women with damaged self-esteem manipulating men, painting them black, and then crying when the connection they share falls apart. Don’t get me wrong, nurse. I am not talking about you, my dear, and I did not mean that you were ungrateful,” Dr. Ade said to the nurse.

“You know my story, so you know who I am referring to. She is just a pretty-faced, big-butted lady who has nothing else to offer. She feels the need to oversee everything, believing that her financial success gives her the upper hand. However, she overlooks the fact that a woman’s pride often comes from having a partner who confidently manages the affairs of their shared life. Any attempt to make her know her place, she calls it abuse; irritatingly being emotional over every damn thing.

“Nonetheless,” Dr. Ade lamented, “we find ourselves in a system where the woman is often deemed to be right, while the man’s need for peace and understanding is frequently overlooked and not regarded as a priority within the marriage or relationship."

"Honestly, I believe that the so-called "good men' often leave us women with little to no choice," the nurse responded, as the apostle quietly observed, allowing the two of them to express their frustrations. "Look at the statistics," she continued, her voice tinged with urgency. "Can't you see how women suffer in relationships? You men often abandon us, leaving us to bear the burdens you created by bringing children into this world without taking responsibility."

The nurse spoke in a low, fervent tone, her fists clenched tightly at her sides, shoulders tense, and eyes narrowed with emotion. As she slowly bowed her head, quiet sobs escaped her lips, filling the heavy silence that enveloped the room.

"Embrace everything you are feeling in this moment and acknowledge the challenges you are facing, your Highness." The apostle said this, tapping the nurse's back gently. "Don't judge it; feel it. Don't resist the feeling, nor feel sorry for yourself, for any act of inner resistance is manure for the ego on which trauma thrives and grows, he assured her. You weep not to show weakness, but because your soul is in dear need of a new experience. It is done sleeping; it is done being bound by ideas, by belief, by a false sense of self and personality. It is done battling wars it knows nothing about; hence, it waves its white flag like silver tears rolling down your cheeks."

"So, tell me, are you not tired of being what you are not? Even actors have moments of respite, and clowns know when to take off their costumes.

When will you learn to respect the moment and listen when the director says 'Cut'?" the apostle said softly to the nurse, whose tears betrayed her struggle. Even the best actors know that the key to a fulfilling stage experience lies in playing their role well. They understand that everything is part of the act and every perception is a tool to enrich the best performance for the audience.

Your teachers, seers, prophets, and societal norms have filled your heart with a script about what defines a virtuous woman and what makes her worthy of her role. Yet, how often has a man been offered a similar script? What truly defines a virtuous man, and what makes him worthy of his part? They seem to overlook a crucial truth: it takes two actors to make the play of eternal union engaging and meaningful.

Have you not been told that two cannot walk together if they disagree? But how can two agree if they do not have the same degree of consciousness? It takes two whole souls to make one. Half-souls live a life in constant search of completion when they should be lovingly living, giving, expressing, and experiencing.

They only take, because for them, giving is synonymous with losing. They have never had anything, so they don't know what it means to give. Have you ever seen beggars who give? They are experts at taking, because lack is a sign of life for their souls. The love of these half-souls who strive for perfection is driven by selfish ideas and plans written by the same directors they perform for. For them, love is a noun, and if love is not protected by names, labels, reasons, and captions, then this love in all its essence is not worth living for. Such love nurtures the ground on which a connection is formed—a connection bound by signatures, written vows, and a plan that governs the experiences of the connection and all that is expressed in it.

You go through existence without loving the other holistically, which is loving exclusively, individualistically, and momentarily, just as people and all of life, with all its imperfections and inconsistencies, should be loved.

Instead, you love as a script created by the system dictates, seeking perfection when progression is the key. Unaware that everything is a performance, many believe that love, like life, requires titles, reasons, vows, and names to be genuine. They feel the need for signatures to validate trust and loyalty. However, true and divine love needs no validation; it simply exists, unwavering and profound, without the need to prove itself.

Besides, what does the air have to prove to the lungs for the lungs to know that the air is what they need to live? Isn't the night sky already all the moon needs to glow? Aren't you the breath in the lungs of the person you say you love? Are you not the moon in their night sky? When will you stop acting to prove and start living to love?" the apostle asked them.

Both Dr. Ade and the nurse remained silent, fully engaged as the apostle spoke, his words weaving a narrative that captured their attention.

"When will you understand time, my beloved? Do you realise that all the relationships you've formed, based on the scripts written by ego-driven influences, are already shaped by the experiences and expectations of those who created them? What you call living and loving is just a performance of their stories.

Who is the director of your soul? What script are you following? Are the voices in your head merely the ones your ego-driven mind is presenting to you, or is it the quieter voice that the same director has labelled as delusional and unconventional, urging you to disregard? The voice of your inner child is quieted by the words it learned to say, the names it was given, the roles it had to play, and the promises it felt it had to make.

The dying voice of your soul longs to be free. It waves its white flags as silver tears roll down your cheeks. Who are you performing for, my beloved? He asked Dr. Ade. Are you acting to be completed, or are you living to experience and express your wholeness?" The apostle asked again, this time looking at the sober nurse.

"Verily, in the heart of the soul that seeks completion, love is war. Loving to such a soul has buried within it the earnest desire to subdue, to win, to conquer, and to own. Such a soul only feels loved when the one it conquers is submissive; hence, in that submission, its ego reigns supreme.

But how can the feminine subdue another if it doesn't first embody masculine traits? Masculine energy, akin to fire, burns brightly, while feminine energy, like water, must first reach a boiling point to be hot enough to burn. How can an eternal union of intimacy thrive when water and fire that should complement each other both burn instead? Yet, they make you boil so much that you forget what it is to be water, and because you have burned for so long, you think you are now on fire. How can a union be full of love when there is a power tussle?

Aye, how treacherous will it be for a starfish to call itself a fish because it lives underwater? Must it have fins, gills, or scales to be considered worthy of being called a fish, or to express itself holistically underwater?

It's a mistake for feminine energy to believe it has to be less feminine to be worthy. Trying to fully express itself doesn't mean it loses its femininity.

You have suppressed your femininity just so that you can burn; can't you see? That is the only way to fight the man—to be of his calibre first. You have grown fins and gills to be called a fish or to be seen as one, though you are a starfish. Life is not a harsh director; it hands each actor a script tailored to their unique abilities. But, how can the actors recognise their abilities if they do not know that they are all actors, and all is play?

The nurse listened soberly and wiped the tears from her cheeks as the apostle turned to Dr. Ade and spoke thus: Did your fathers not pass down to you the knowledge I taught them? Did they not instruct you that what takes two to make also takes two to nurture? Who made you, Lord, to decree that two captains cannot be on the same ship? When did setting the course and steering the ship become a war? Who made it a competition? Why can't two captains steer a single ship? Do you not know that collaboration is life and work made easy? Have you not heard the wisdom of your prophets? For in this life, every man is a farmer, tilling the soil of dreams, while every woman is the land, nurturing the seeds of life and love.

What land is fertile and fruitful that has not been weeded and tended by the diligent farmer? What seed, I ask, can blossom into a mighty tree without the farmer's tender care—with their watering, pruning, and nurturing hands? What tree can thrive without the rich soil that cradles its roots, nurtured by the sunlight of passion and the rain of devotion, to bear the bountiful fruits of life.

What tree grows and bears tasty fruit if the farmer wages war on the land where the tree is planted? Are the trees not the bearers of pain, and their growth stunted when the land in which they are rooted and the farmers are at war? Can the land cultivate itself? Can the farmer birth trees? Yet, you fight for titles, promises, and unions made of nouns, for your feeble vows, and for a love that is scripted and acted upon.

Aye, the land and the farmer must be in divine harmony so that healthy trees are born and nurtured to fruitfulness and healthy growth. The tree would always be dry and leafless in summer, when it was supposed to blossom, because the farmer who was supposed to water and prune it was absent. Now the land ploughs itself, and the farmer feels useless, and his role in the game of intimacy is threatened.

"Verily, I say to you, like the dying voice that speaks within you, and inflicts pain on you just to wake you up. I speak to you like the voice that wants you to know your place, O woman, as Mother Earth. It is like the faint voice that urges you to take your place as a farmer, oh man. This is the inner voice that is shackled by ideas and conventional thoughts that wants to break free. It is the voice that wants to remind you that life is a play and you should act according to the script it serves you, but you neglect it because the script does not feel familiar.

This divine script is characterised by elements of emotional intelligence, acceptance, vulnerability, attraction, healthy connection, collaboration, and a diligent commitment to service. It inspires us to live in the moment, all rooted in love and a sense of oneness."

The apostle rose and faced them, his eyes seasoned with knowledge and his tongue raining truth in the form of words that moistened their dry souls as they listened, spellbound, to every word he spoke.

"Authenticity is the costume you must wear as you play the script that life has written in your heart while performing momentarily on the ethereal stage of love in the theatre of divine union. Conventional thinking has locked the doors of this theatre with keys made of illusory promises and negative beliefs. Trying to play roles other than your true nature as a farmer and your universal essence as land will only lead to conflict. However, when two souls dance in a state of self-awareness and self-expression, a beautiful union blossoms.

The stage is illuminated with joy and self-realisation. Being true to oneself is the most captivating performance a soul can offer, where two hearts harmonise effortlessly on the cosmic stage of divine union. In this love-filled union, a seed is planted, nurtured, and grown into a tree whose fruit tastes sweeter than fine wine and whose leaves bring healing beyond any herb.

Heaven knows how this man knows all that he says, Dr. Ade thought to himself as the apostle ceased speaking. Both of them took a moment to absorb the weight of the apostle's words, and within that silence, they made a profound discovery.

Their expressions mirrored the epiphanies they had just encountered, as if a fog had lifted, revealing a landscape of truth newly brought into view.

"Thank you for the medication; I feel better now," said the apostle to the nurse, who was still sitting there in awe. "No one has ever spoken to me in such a way as to make my soul feel naked and vulnerable," she replied. "I should thank you for your kind words; I am glad this moment happened.

You are welcome, Your Highness," replied the apostle. "But I am most grateful to you for spending your time listening to a schizophrenic old man share his delusions with you." He said to her with a grin on his face as he calmly made his way to the door.

"I think I have to go to my room and rest a bit." The apostle said to Dr. Ade as he made his way out. "The medication is making me feel sleepy."

"What about your meal that is being heated for you?" Dr. Ade asked, walking behind him. "I don't feel hungry anymore. You can make me a cup of tea; it will be enough for now." The Apostle replied.

"Fair enough, you have a big day ahead; your tribunal is coming up soon, so you need to rest and get prepared, Mr. Abdul Malik," Dr. Ade said.

"All is well," replied the apostle with a smile as he walked into his room, shutting the door behind him.

ETERNAL DENOUEMENTS IN TRANSIENT EXPOSITIONS

"Excuse me, sister, do you have a minute? I need a cup of coffee and two cubes of sugar, please." The patient asked, walking past the nurse into the garden as she went down the corridor and to the apostle's room to serve him his cup of tea.

"Here we go, Apostle; I have made it the way you like it, with milk and no sugar." She said to the apostle as she walked into his room with the door wide open. "Sorry, I forgot to knock," she pleaded. "That's no problem, Your Highness.

I knew you would bring a cup of tea, so I left the door open. I will let the tea cool down a little before I take a sip; I don't want to burn my tongue on the piping hot brew." He replied with a cheerful grin.

"Do not worry; take your time," said the nurse with a beaming smile on her face. "Um, I don't want to bother you, Apostle; it's just that after what you said a few moments ago, I haven't been able to settle down. Maybe that's how it is when you start to let go of what you have been used to all your life.

But yes, I am infinitely grateful. It's really funny, but I realised that no one knows everything. Who would have imagined that the event that would profoundly alter the course of my life would originate from a patient in a place as unassuming as this? Now I understand why diamonds are found in the rough." She said to the apostle, who just stared at her with a smile hidden under his thick moustache as she continued speaking.

"But something still plagues my heart. The words you said about us being actors are what I have been trying to make sense of. I know this might not be the right time for this, and I know that you are probably tired and ready to call it a day," she remarked. "But please, I don't want to lose this moment, because I believe the clarity that I need can only be experienced right now.

I am fully convinced that your admission here is no coincidence. Deep down, there has always been a part of me that believes this. There has always been this thing inside me that is convinced. Where I come from in Nigeria, it is called a 'body tell,' and that body tell doesn't lie to me. I might not know your real name or anything about you, but I know that you are not just here because of any mentally related thing; it was divinely orchestrated. I wasn't supposed to be on shift today, but for some reason, here I am. So, please, can you explain to me what you meant when you said we are all actors? Because in my head, I feel that being an actor is saying one shouldn't be real. Acting is a form of make-believe, and if the essence of existence lies in authenticity, doesn't seeing myself as an actor contradict what it truly means to live?" the nurse asked, her curiosity evident.

The apostle stared at her for a few seconds and replied thus: "Are we not the best form of entertainment for another? Are you not role-playing in all your daily lives? You seldom and creatively strive to play the role of a good mother; you play the role of a good human. You also play the role of a good nurse.

How, then, do you wonder? Can't you see that your struggle with yourself and the role you are meant to play is linked to a misunderstanding of the script? You're not actively and diligently interpreting the roles assigned to you. Are you, therefore, not the actor and director of your fate in every scene life serves you momentarily? Isn't the entertainment value of each scene—whether it's engaging or dull—dependent on your willingness to accept and interpret your role per the script tailored for that moment?

Aye, don't you, like many screenwriters, craft the scripts and roles that you and others are meant to play in every moment, labelling them with the grand title of "expectations'? Don't the haunting shadows of past roles influence the scripts and delivery of your current roles in such a way that you try to play better in your current scripts to make up for the roles you didn't play well in the past?

Aren't you a prisoner of the role you feel good, comfortable, and stuck in because it's all you know, and every attempt to try a new and unfamiliar role feels like you're languishing in hell?" The apostle asked her.

"Truly, the salvation your soul longs for is exclusively written in bold fonts on the pages of your heart. It is an act of delusion for one actor to ask another actor if they are actors in the play in which they both play parts."

The nurse stood there again, stunned and speechless, staring at the apostle with wide eyes. The apostle stood up, went to the table in his room, opened a poetry book on the table titled, 'For Broken Vessels' written by Victor Kwesi, took out a neatly folded white sheet of paper, approached the nurse, and handed her the paper. She took the paper, stared at it, and put it in the pocket of the tunic she was wearing. "Thank you, Apostle; I will be sure to read what's on the paper when I get to the office," she said, turning and walking calmly to the door and out of the apostle's room.

"When she arrived at the staff office," she sat down, reached into her pocket, pulled out the paper, and lo and behold, it was a beautifully crafted piece. It was written with the best writing she had ever seen from a resident in all the years she had worked in the mental health industry. The poem read thus:

"Life is the theatre.

Each moment is a scene to be lived on the stage called existence.

The spotlight is on you, the main character,

prepared to enchant the hearts of those eager for a transformative journey into the realms of imagination and emotion.

Living is a divine act of role-playing,

interpreting scripts written with the ink of self-expression and living experiences.

The first scene begins with the character crying.

The last scene ends with the character dying.

All are nothing but entertainers.

Some are underpaid actors.

Some are overpaid actors.

Some are bold and cocky; their egos are always on the flight.

Some try to fight stage fright; their tool is getting high, and that makes them feel alright.

Some try not to even try; their claim is; they are shy.

Some get bored when there is no ovation,

hence, besotted with thoughts of past performances.

How poignant and extremely piteous they are;

they don't notice time passing them by.

Some get so attached while watching the actors perform.

They judge and compare when the actors come on,

and cry when they are gone.

The backstage for actors is the womb.

The offstage is the tomb.

In the same room, we are all gathered, playing characters

while being the audience too.

Am I entertained?

Oh, yes!

And you?

Are you expressing and experiencing?

Or do you enjoy judging the character

so much that your attention is now stuck on comparison like glue?

You call them boring when you get familiar with the character.

But how do their souls feed if you don't cheer, adore, and affirm the character?

Don't you know that love fuels the character?

And love is the character's essence?

Non is a better character, but comparison makes it so.

No act is a good or bad act, but expectation makes it so.

We are all acting; our souls are directing.

Sadly, these directors steal your soul,

their scripts, you now live and sleep on.

Some are still asleep; some are lucid dreaming.

But the main show begins when you realise

that reality is only a dream,

the very moment the director yells "cut."

The nurse read and smiled, folded the paper, and tucked it right back in her pocket. Serendipity, she muttered to herself.

"Hm, who wrote you a love letter that put a smile on your face?" asked Dr. Ade, who was sitting next to her.

"That's none of your business," she said, giggling.

"Do you ever believe in divine timing, Doc?" she asked Dr. Ade.

"Well, it depends, but yes, I do," he replied.

"The thing is, I feel like everything that's been happening lately has been happening in divine timing. I am here to experience it all," she said.

"So, are you going in with the apostle tomorrow for his tribunal?" she asked Dr Ade.

"Well, I could, if the powers that be do not change things. But it will be difficult because I don't have much personal information about him. But he told me his name was Abdul Malik. Honestly, I don't even know if I should believe that," he replied.

"You should just believe what he said since there is no evidence. He doesn't even have a passport or any other means of identification. So just go by what he told you his name was," the nurse explained.

We'll see how it goes tomorrow; I will always think of something. I just do not think he should be here anymore. This place is not right for him. This old man is light-years ahead of everyone here," replied Dr. Ade.

"But don't forget he's schizophrenic," said the doctor, who had been sitting unnoticed at the end of the hall during the event, absorbing everything the apostle said. He relayed this information to the management. The doctor, in his mid-30s, was from North London but of Sudanese origin, and was seated next to the door, working on his computer and occasionally interrupting their conversation.

"But who isn't, though?" Dr. Ade asked in reply to the Doctor.

"That's not the point, mate," replied the British-born Sudanese doctor. "I am just saying that your supposed apostle, usually lost in his schizophrenic musings, is fast becoming a nuisance in this ward with his rants and misguided statements that you have all mistakenly accepted as the divine truth. I have seen you all fall for the delusions he mentioned during the event. You, of all people, should have known better, Dr. Ade. You are a mental health doctor and should be able to recognise delusions better than anyone. Well, I am glad it's coming to an end," he said haughtily.

"I know you never liked him, but what do you mean?" asked Dr. Ade curiously.

"We'd be better off if he were not causing trouble with his delusional stories. He has to go; that's all I am saying," the doctor asserted. "He has no known name and not even a legal identity. Sometimes I get the feeling he could be one of those refugees from war-torn countries in Africa who find themselves in the streets causing trouble in town centres," he said superciliously.

Dr Ade replied: "He may speak in riddles, but there is wisdom in his words. He's completely harmless, and the patients find comfort in his presence. Since he has been here, the ward has "become very quiet. The other patients complain of boredom less often than before, because he is constantly engaging them in healthy conversations, no matter how delusional the stories he shares with them may sound, and you know how much integration helps patients calm down. Don't you think that sending him away now could upset the delicate balance of his rehabilitation and the healing of the other patients?

Wisdom? sneered the Sudanese doctor. It's all garbage. We're here to provide stability and support to patients, not to listen to the vagaries and deluded idiosyncrasies of a confused mind. We will be setting ourselves and this facility up for ruin if he stays. After my discussion with management regarding everything he said during the event and how much the patients now regard him as their saviour, I will accompany him to his tribunal tomorrow."

"That is crazy," Dr. Ade replied. Firm in his stance, he retorted, "We're healers, not judges. Every voice here matters. Maybe, just maybe, the apostle's words hold a key to unlocking someone else's healing. Let's not dismiss the unknown so easily. I knew that was your plan all along of representing him tomorrow was to make sure he leaves. . But yeah, good luck with that!"

"This conversation is getting boring," the Nigerian nurse interrupted. "Kudos to whoever is going to stand for the apostle tomorrow. As for me, I can't wait for you to hand over to the person on the night shift. It feels like a big burden has been lifted off my chest today. I feel a lot lighter, to be honest. Today has been a great day, so I can't wait to get home, get cosy, and have a movie night with my little man."

"Are you talking about the man who wrote you the love letter, the one that got you smiling from ear to ear?" Dr. Ade asked sarcastically. Hahaha, the nurse laughed out loud. "Maybe, you can never tell," she replied. I meant, my son, you nasty-minded man, she said again, laughing out loud.

“Well, you deserve it. I will meet you at the handover room then,” Dr. Ade said as he walked out of the office.

BROKEN BREAD AND SPILLED WINE

May I come in?" Dr. Ade asked as he knocked. "Sure, you are welcome, Doc," replied the apostle.

"I was just leaving because the night member of staff has just arrived, so I thought I should inform you of the latest developments regarding your tribunal tomorrow.

Dr. Ade cleared his throat, his eyes fixed on the apostle. "I have to be honest with you, Apostle. I will not be able to attend your tribunal, and, well, who knows how it will turn out?"

The apostle met Doctor Ade's gaze with a calm nod. ""Make no mistake; life is a series of tribunals," he replied. "And I have had my share of them. Sometimes, you have to stand alone.

Maybe tomorrow is one of those moments. But I know that in those moments, your truth and the echoes of your personality are heard the loudest. I know how hard you try to help me and make sure I don't leave and return to the cold streets."

Dr. Ade felt the weight of the apostle's response and the conflict with his good intentions to ensure fair treatment during the tribunal. He realised that perseverance in the face of uncertainty can be a quiet victory in a well-lived life. "Well, I will be on my way now. As you always used to say, all is well."

"Indeed, all is well, Doc," replied the apostle with a bold grin on his face. "Enjoy your long holiday, because I may not be here when you come back, to tell me all the things you have done and the women you have been with," the apostle said, chuckling.

"That would be sad, but thank you for reminding me," replied Dr. Ade, taking out a notebook and pen.

"Why the notebook and pen?" asked the apostle, staring at Dr. Ade.

"Nothing really serious," replied the doctor. "I just need something to keep. I have heard you talking the whole time. I have internalised your words, every single one, but I think others need to hear them too. I am working on a book right now, and if you don't mind, I'd be happy if you'd leave me something to share."

"Words mean nothing, Doc," the apostle replied. "All I can say are just words, my experiences, and nothing more. We all walk different paths, and the maps are different too."

"I understand all this, but what use is the wisdom of the elders if their experience is not used as a light to guide the young to follow their path efficiently? So, all I ask for is the light, not just for me, but for anyone who wants to experience the book I am working on. I know you need to rest for your big day tomorrow, but if that's all I can get, I'd be very grateful," pleaded Dr. Ade.

The apostle was silent for more than three minutes and then spoke thus: "These keys that I share with you today open up realms beyond the visible," the apostle replied. "Remember to keep them sacred, for they connect not only to unknown doors but also to mind, heart, body, and soul. Listen with the heart, internalise with the mind, examine with the spirit, accept with the soul, and write it down so that souls may come to light through inner remembrance once they experience it."

Dr. Ade rose from the edge of the bed on which he was sitting, drew the empty chair in the middle of the room closer to the bed, and sat down opposite the apostle. His book rested on his thigh, his heart open to receive, his soul vulnerable to evolve, and his right hand ready to write down whatever the apostle had to say.

"As you now sit down to note all that is to be drawn from the apostle's well, see to it that you also make a conscious inventory of what you give and share the most, for this tells you in detail what you lack and what you need. So, exhort all liberal hearts and generous souls to always remember that every gift is a mirror for self-reflection. Everything that is given is a subtle cry for what the giver needs.

To those who are hasty in spirit, you will give these words. Those who hunt for the meaning of life instead of living life meaningfully: remind them that the mind lacks nothing except what it is convinced it needs but does not have. The dreaded fear of missing out is merely a thought born of the conviction that now is not enough. Let them know that life is best experienced urgently and not hastily, and that this is what it is meant to be. The acceptance of the moment is the key to the door that leads to self-sufficiency.

Let the soul that earnestly seeks know that the more it loves, adores, worships, and cherishes its true self, the more it will attract the soul that will also adore, worship, and love its genuineness. But if it repels itself, it will never attract the right other. Recognising and attracting the right other depends solely on self-awareness, which is the image and revelation of God in self.

To all warriors of life, this light you shall minister to their darkened hearts. Souls who fight to feel accepted, who fight to feel whole, and who battle to feel loved. So, they will remember that what doesn't kill them will not make them stronger, but will only traumatise them. It is the momentary acceptance and healing of the trauma that will ultimately make them stronger.

To the supposed gatekeepers of heaven and judges of the universe: they judge every action and condemn every word. They define what a sin is, who is condemned by God, and who is embraced by Him.

Teach them that if there's a list of sins against God, using His name carelessly won't be on it. A name is just a label; it only highlights the true meaning behind it. At the top of this eternal list, then, would be the heretical act of doubting one's abilities and genius, for when one doubts oneself, God is tamed. To be God is to be wild, and to be God-loving rather than God-fearing is to be free.

To all time-keepers and ardent workers: Blessed are those who understand time and do not seek to possess it, for heaven is theirs to dwell in every moment. May they be so transformed that they realise that idleness is not synonymous with rest.

Rest is the reward of work done, and idleness is the reward for work not done. Let them know that all prayer is work fuelled by deliberate planning, process addiction, and results-oriented abstinence. Words are the bricks and mortar from which our wishes and dreams are built, while praise serves as the fuel that feeds the ego."

All these tools and materials are essential for constructing a fulfilling life. However, it is work—the creative integration of these tools—when aligned with love and time, that brings the divine to life.

Let them also remember to carry this awareness close to their hearts: some die too soon while working tirelessly, while others pass away too late, caught in idleness. True divinity lies in those who depart at the right time, for they leave this world empty of unfulfilled dreams, vibrant and alive, even in old age."

To the souls who perceive the glorious act of feeling as vulnerability and vulnerability as weakness: minister to them and remind them that the greatest act of righteousness for a living being is to feel. To fully and deeply embrace whatever emotions arise in the moment—be it love, pain, fear, happiness, sadness, joy, or sorrow.

To feel an emotion fully—without judging it, suppressing it, or comparing it—is to allow vulnerability. And it is in that vulnerability that God can fully express Himself.

To hearts conditioned to see sweetness and softness as the root of attraction, teach them that upon awakening, they should remember that the sweetest berries that are eaten the most while the softest hearts are the most fragile. In the world that craves sweetness and softness, being like water is all they need to be—tasteless yet so nourishing, formless yet gentle.

To all universal actors and actresses who perform creatively and diligently in the theatre called existence, entertaining the audience with their every role: remember, before stepping on any stage, that the root of all suffering lies in the non-mastery of times and seasons. It's like wearing armour to sleep and pyjamas to war. Life moments are stages, and you are always in the spotlight. So, remember to wear the right costume for the role you are playing.

Share the good news with the weary at heart, with the souls who weep ceaselessly, for their heartbeats echo with longsuffering. They wail, believing their struggles pale in comparison to others' lives. Remind them that every curse casts a shadow of blessings, and every deity harbours a devil within its ego. Let them remember that we are all interconnected. Even the rich man, in his abundance, is profoundly poor, forever desiring, wanting, and seeking to possess.

To the philosophers who search for the meaning of life in thoughts, tell them not to forget that in every child lies an old man, just as in every cradle lies a grave. The end is revealed in the beginning, just as a new birth is proof of the certainty of death. Life can often seem meaningless. When we seek to give it meaning, we risk crafting a version of God that is limited by personality traits. Such a diminished deity, defined by our weaknesses, can lead to a rather bleak existence. Instead of confining God to our human understanding, we might find greater depth in embracing the mysteries of life itself.

To the souls who patiently walk through dark tunnels and hope to meet the light at the end, remind them to no longer hope in vain, for they are light enough. Only when they turn on their light within will their path be illuminated, for the tunnel is only an illusion created by the lack of light.

To the warlords with their arsenals filled with weapons made of prayer requests and prayer points: aye, they are the target audience of the hope and miracle peddlers. Do well to remind them that the miracle they are praying, fighting, casting, binding, and believing God for is in the work they are ceaselessly avoiding.

Tell them to stop praying when they can, for I tell you again, as I also reminded your fathers, that diligent work done in love and guided by good intentions is the greatest act of hope, faith, and prayer there is. And what is diligence, if not work done—done when it should be, for the right purpose, through love and with love?

Let them not forget that sand has lost its value through its sheer simplicity and familiarity, much like the divine sense we call "common,' which many souls find themselves drowning in amid the tides of conventional thought. This so-called common sense is, in fact, a rare plant. Yet, everyone carries its seed within. How tragic it is that the judges and lawmakers of the universe now depend on the very vices they once condemned as profane and vain. These things have become the fragile keys to their sanity. Therefore, remind them not to be quick to judge or label, lest they become the very thing they quickly condemn.

Share this guiding light with all those who seek friendship and the comforting embrace of companionship, ensuring they do not linger in eternal darkness. Remind them that with the gift of friendship often comes the emergence of an adversary.

Prosperity breeds fear. The wind nurtures trees in spring. It transforms them in summer with melodies, making the branches dance. But come autumn, it strips them bare. For when the heart chooses friends carefully, it offers them the keys to its soul. They enter and exit as they wish.

Life, they say, is love, and love is life. So, tell these words to all seekers of life who sincerely pursue love. Let them hear these words: Many know of love, but few truly embrace it. The gods among them are those who manifest love in their actions. For what is divinity if not love in motion? Admonish them never to forget that while many may coexist in love, few are those who strive to truly feel the depths of what love offers

The true gods among them are those who actively create the love they wish to experience. For what is creation but the pure, divine act of expressing Godliness?

Let the light of truth shine on their faces, so that their souls may remember not to forget that many pray for a love so pure and true. Few are those who wait patiently for a love so pure and so true. But the true gods are those who embody, cultivate, and experience the love in its truest form. What, after all, is love in its eternal essence if not the force that breaks the shackles preventing the divine from fully manifesting?

To the few who are willing to lose themselves and become one with love, these words shall you share with them proportionally. Constantly remind them that many are those who serve in love, yet few truly open themselves to receive it vulnerably.

The true gods are those who embrace an eternal emptiness for love, for what purpose is a vessel of love if it is always full?

Do not forget to reach out to souls who constantly chase after love, for in their deluded expectations, love is only a reward. Do not shy away from reminding them that their hearts tirelessly chase after love, not out of a genuine desire for love itself, but for the sweet rewards and feelings that accompany it.

Truly, love is not merely a reward; it is a sacred calling, guiding us toward a deeper self-awareness and allowing for authentic self-expression that transcends the confines of the ego.

Dr. Ade wrote incessantly, and when the apostle was about to utter his next words, he raised his head and asked him thus, "What about those who have loved deeply and endured the pain of loss? How do entwined hearts heal after a loss? They awaken to a symphony of regret, transforming shadows of the past into glowing memories. In shared vulnerability, they turn grief into golden echoes, guiding them toward renewal.

The apostle paused for a few seconds, took a deep breath, exhaled slowly, adjusted himself on the bed, and replied to him, saying, "A heart that needs healing is a heart that is broken.

That which the soul calls heartbreak is only the death of its ego, powered by illusory expectations. Therefore, remind such souls that nothing is ever lost. An experience that has met its end doesn't mean the death or end of love.

A soul that turns a blind eye to the value of its experiences often misses the profound beauty woven into both their beginnings and endings. Yet, when this soul awakens to the bittersweet truth that every moment is bound by time's gentle embrace, it begins to treasure each fleeting expression of love.

In this realisation, it learns to dance with the ephemeral, savouring every shared glance and whispered word, before they dissolve into the tapestry of memory, forever etched in the heart.

Those who inflict deep wounds upon themselves are often the first to perceive their worthlessness and emptiness. They feel unworthy of love and connection, lamenting, "No one can truly value me, for I am broken." Their cries echo a profound sadness, a yearning for healing that seems just out of reach. Hence, "Only a skilled mechanic or a true saviour can pull them from the brink.

Remind them gently that no one is truly damaged and no one is bound; therefore, no one requires repairs. What the mind perceives as damage is merely the veil that shrouds and suppresses the self. In truth, it is the act of remembering that offers the healing these souls seek."

Once the soul can come to the light of self-awareness through remembering, the veil is lifted. What was once perceived as damage or brokenness begins to serve as a portal through which the enlightened light within passes to illuminate the world outside of the self. Even scars like happy faces are medals for life lived and experiences gained.

To those awakened souls who recognise that self-expression is at the heart of life, encourage them to continue sharing and embracing every moment, unapologetically. Remind them that for those driven by ego, self-expression can feel like a transgression. To these minds, a person brimming with life and laughter, without the need for a comedian, might be seen as unhinged. In their eyes, true sanity and maturity mean enduring a life rife with misery and suffering.

To those who are so quick to sing the songs of sad birds, pity seekers, singing their best songs to attract sympathy, do well to pass this little guiding light to them. In vain it is to sing the hymns of the hopeless, the sad tune of regret, the cries of a life not lived, and dreams not realised.

Remind them that the worst pang of conscience is that which ends with the heart-wrenching aphorism, 'I just had to settle for it'. Anything settled for is a thing that has been drained of hope, love, and truth.

To the minds shaped by the relentless rhetoric of hope-sellers and the numbing whispers of attention-seekers, tell them to remember to trust their feelings and embrace them. They should not succumb to the pressure to fight against or suppress your emotions. Instead, honour their vice and allow it to guide them. Do well to urge them to tear away the veil of rigidity that blinds their consciousness. Remind them that just because a thing is felt does not make it real, for fear is the proof of this truth.

To avid lovers, with their sharp swords, ready to dissect love into its various parts: they are creatively astute, eager to label and cherish each piece with its unique language. Remind them that love is best experienced whole, for love doesn't live through a source. It fears no lack. It is the source; hence, it doesn't need to speak in multiple languages to be understood. Neither does it need different titles and captions to be expressed or experienced.

Guide these lovers through remembrance, I beseech you, so they will remember not to forget that if love should ever have a language, then attention would certainly be what its mother tongue would be. For whatever the soul is attentive to, it loves ceaselessly and rightly.

Some live life feeling indebted to it; they don't express themselves. Life must sort them out before they do. Some live thinking they owe life. Hence, they live life trying to please it. Some find themselves drowning in the limiting consciousness that the reward of a pleasing life is happiness. How weary their joy has become; how sad their reality is!

Remind such souls that life never promised happiness as a reward for pleasing it or as a prize for entitlement. All it promised were momentary experiences, and the breath to create these experiences through self-expression. Living means creatively expressing who you are. "Life unfolds like a vibrant canvas, and when we dive into its colours, happiness dances around us—an enchanting prize for our heartfelt artistry."

To those who create, help them remember this: to create is to fully exist. Art born of time requires time to breathe. When art emerges beyond the confines of time, it becomes divine.

Therefore, its existence is eternal, for things of high quality and inestimable value have no fear of time. Its lifespan transcends time, for it was created outside of time.

To the dreamers who tirelessly seek a Joseph to interpret their dreams like a beloved sport: remember that each dream, with its individuality and uniqueness, can only be understood by the dreamer themselves. Just as a vision can only be fully realised by the visionary, so too must they embrace the interpretation of their dreams as a personal journey. There are no saviours outside themselves; for all are to themselves saviours.

The work of growth and healing must be done from within, and any praise for that work ultimately belongs to them. Everything is interconnected, and at the heart of it all is the self, powered by the very breath of life. And may they also embrace this truth: that they are both the authors of our journeys and the divine energy propelling them forward.

To those who are so quick to seek opposites in everything, wholeness may appear as a challenge to their understanding, and embracing a balanced perspective can seem like a lack of passion. Yet, true wisdom often resides in the middle ground, where extremes fade and a deeper understanding flourishes. In the quest for the false peace of being "different,' some people cling tightly to one extreme while hurling insults at the other. They don't see that there are simply two sides of the same coin. Let's remind these souls that they are all birds of a feather, connected in our humanity. Instead of being trapped in conventional thinking, let them soar together by celebrating their differences. When they embrace diversity, they can rise above division and comparison, transforming discord into harmony.

To intelligent minds, certainty is a cue before life can be experienced. For them, if life isn't figured out completely, then there seems to be no point in living it. Remind such a soul that the juice of life is drained out of life when the goal shifts to figuring out moments instead of simply living them.

No one can perceive the end of life's moment from the beginning thereof, not even life itself, for life has no beginning or end. The beauty of living is understanding that moments are mysteries to be, much like a book waiting to be read. When they embrace a moment fully, they allow the mystery to unfurl, revealing its joys and insights only after they've truly loved it.

To the hearts that beat in time, shall you surely serve this soulful reminder that breathing heals all pain, not time. Even time is essential, only in the presence of breath. Besides, what use is time if there is no life to give it meaning?" the apostle asked.

Dr. Ade was puzzled and had no answer to give. He stopped writing, raised his head, stared at the apostle, and replied, "To be honest, I never thought about it until this moment. I have always believed in the adage that time is everything, but now I have realised that time means nothing to a dead man." The apostle smiled at him, got up from his bed, walked to the table. Dr. Ade just watched, took a sip from the cold cup of tea on the table, walked back to the bed, sat down, and continued talking.

"To all orators and warriors of light, whose swords are pens and shields made of paper, dauntlessly do they war against rigid hearts. Tirelessly, they speak their truth and bare their souls. Do well, therefore, to remind them to be good storytellers. Urge them to create those mental pictures that are not as though they were. They should effortlessly sell fish to the sea, heat to the sun, sand to the desert, and make stones soft, allowing dark souls to shine bright like diamonds.

Tell all these lovers, who dance in the shadows of half-baked love, composed of comparisons, judgments, and illusory expectations, to awaken to the truth. Encourage them to sift through the clutter of their hearts and discard everything that is not love from the nourishing feast they serve one another.

Let them savour only the pure ingredients of authentic connection, seasoning their bond with trust, compassion, and understanding, so that their love can truly flourish and inspire. Remind them thoroughly that true beauty is perceived in the moment when the sense of comparison and familiarity takes its last breath. True love is experienced the moment the thought of reasons, comparisons, judgments, and illusory expectations cease to exist.

You will sternly instruct all rumour-mongers to refrain from spreading the falsehood that the love of money is the root of all evil. Aye, remind them that love has no bidding with evil, and evil does not rule with love. For an ego-ridden spirit, bereft of joy, is the root that bears the trunk, branch, leaves, and fruit of the tree called evil. To all the soldiers of faith who are heavily armed and on the lookout for devils to fight and kill, remind them warmly that man is the devil behind his troubles, God behind his miracles, and the body in the middle experiencing the extremes.

To souls who live hastily, this piece of light shall you joyfully serve them. Patience is torture for such souls, and to wait for them is to die. Remind them that looking at the clock will only make their hearts suffer, and counting miles will only make their eyes bitter.

To the watchmen who wait with fervent hearts for the hand of God in their pursuits: Aye, in vain they watch, for their waiting bears the weight of futility. Let it be known to such souls that with every thought that blossoms into reality, the hand of God is woven into the very fabric of its creation. Whether it be for good or ill, nothing comes to fruition without the gift of breath. For breath is the supreme expression of the divine, the very hand of God guiding our existence.

To those who selfishly pray for a life without pain and strife, wishing for long sunny days and summer that never sees winter, remember this: life is like the clouds. Some days are dark, grey, stormy, and gloomy. Some days are sunny and white, with a touch of blue. It's all part of the journey, and it's through these challenges that we truly grow. The more man prays, the more life laughs. Verily, some days bring pain; some days bring unspeakable joy, but every day remains a day, just as every cloud, whether dark or white, remains a cloud.

For those souls who have made comparison a sign of life, to such souls, nothing is, until it is compared to what is supposed to be. Strive to remind them to be careful that they do not miss life by listening to the noise of comparison. That which they call a shape is only a form of line. That which they call darkness is only a gradation of light. That which they perceive as tall or mock as short is only a form of height, and what they call ugly is only a form of beauty. For in the end, everything is the same, and life knows no difference, only the variety of sameness.

Woe unto the soul that is quick to label life based on a momentary experience, for with sadness and grief will such a soul break bread continually. Remind such souls to accept life momentarily, because that which they label and call good and evil is only the fruit of their understanding.

For the wedding planner, rain is an obstacle and a source of pain, but for the farmer, it is the answer to his prayers and a divine source of joy and growth. Blessed are those who are like the farmer, for every experience, both good and bad, will cultivate growth and bring forth blessings to nurture what they are sowing in their lives.

To the ultimate seekers on a quest for realisation, remember this: in the act of searching through every reflection, it is in vain to seek your true essence if you fear to let go of the self you cling to. Embrace the journey with courage, for self-discovery often requires shedding the familiar. To lose oneself is to lose the idea of self, which is not the true self but only a shadow of it. The clouds lose themselves to make rain. The seed loses itself to make a tree. The egg relinquishes its form to give rise to new beings. Aye, how ignorant will it be for humans to cling to their ego-curated idea of self for fear of losing self, yet losing self and still not finding their true essence?

To the men of the cloth who parade as shepherds, asserting ownership of words and dishing out laws to be adhered to and rules to follow, all for breadcrumbs in heaven and mansions in Nirvana, remind such men that: all conventions moral codes, and symbols are man-made. All they hold dear is shaped by thought. Even their concepts of God and the Devil are reflections of humanity, crafted in our image and likeness. What man has created, he can also control and ultimately destroy.

To light bearers, those to whom the torch of enlightenment has been entrusted may they not shrink in trepidation, even when darkness rages against their glow.

Remind them ardently to learn from the candle. Its light so bright doth shine, its wax so hot it burns; it understands what living purpose entails. It understands that to truly shine is to truly die, and to love and live purposefully is to ebulliently end oneself. Oh, what joy it is to die for that which one lives for! In the end, the essence of purpose is to embrace death for its sake. Only then can one truly live purposefully, embodying the meaning that drives us.

To all who wear the label of scepticism around their necks: your minds may be shackled by, and your souls confined. Your ego thrives in the superficial act of illusory knowledge. Remind yourselves of this truth that surpasses all doubt: to love is to be consciously open to the possibility of being broken.

To rejoice in the bliss of rain is to plunge with joy onto muddy roads. Knowledge, in all its ego-driven divinity, prides itself as the fork in the road that leads to wisdom. Yet even those who are ignorant and walk the same path can sometimes be considered wise.

To self-harmers whose life purpose is to suppress their inner child, they blame themselves for the sake of others, and harm themselves for the attention and sympathy of others. They live like vultures, feeding on dead things just to prove that they are mature. They experiment with drugs, just to get high above the sky, with the intent of meeting the Lord, but only end up in psychiatric wards, while blaming it on the illusory pursuit of joy.

Such souls will yet be reminded that suppression of the inner child is the death of the soul, and the pursuit of happiness is as endless as life itself. The joy they seek and the happiness they crave have never been outside of self but within self, buried in the heart of the inner child that they have been suppressing.

To the souls that pride themselves on aloneness, the ones whose heaven is found in seclusion: they wear independence as gold chains around their necks and tags of isolation as bracelets around their wrists. Remind such souls that the universe thrives not in isolation, for nothing is ever isolated. Verily, these little guiding lights, so sad, yet so true. No matter how much they now live on labels, beliefs, and ideas, when old age calls, when beauty fades, and their skin gets intimate with wrinkles, their souls will yearn for a radiant heart to ignite their spirits. They will yearn for devoted companions to embrace them through life's tempestuous storms.

To all clowns, boors, and nomads traipsing the earth, do gleefully remind them that the universe, in its benevolence, bears no grudge and has no judgement against its vessels. Some radiate joy wherever they go, while others cast a lingering sense of judgment in their wake as they depart. Buried in each vessel are their judge, advocate, and prosecutor. Their choices are their testaments, and their conscience is the courtroom.

Do not forget the divine tramps and spiritual vagrants; they live life sending messages to heaven for things they have but think they lack. Aye, even the heavens will have their ears filled with their prayers and requests. Their prayers are not found in heaven or resting in the palms of God; they are rather buried in their choices.

Do well to remind them to slow down and appreciate that which they have but don't realise they need, and that which they need but fail to realise that they already have. They have two hands to build all that they dream of and pray about."

The Apostle stood up from the bed where he sat, walked close to Dr Ade, placed his right hand on his right shoulder, stared at him for a few seconds, and asked him calmly.

"How drunk is your soul from the wine the apostle has poured into your conscience? How well fed is your heart from the bread that we have been breaking?" Dr. Ade, with his eyes wide open and his mouth slightly ajar, like he had seen a ghost, was terrified to speak. All he did was just sit and stare at the apostle.

"These last words do I leave you with, my beloved friend," the apostle continued. "For tomorrow, the apostle will return to whence he came.

As you breathe, so will your heart desire, and endlessly will your soul want. But endeavour to always audit your soul, for sometimes the things you feel you want and need are birthed out of lack, buried unhealed traumas, low self-esteem, and sheer insecurities.

Sadly, as it is, don't be like the men of the world who crave normality, for all of life for them is an endless chase of an illusory sense of perfection. How pathetic is the chase! Even life itself has imperfection as its core element of beauty.

Therefore, I urge you, like I did your prophets and fathers, to make progression your only chase, for only in progression can perfection be lived and experienced. And in all that ye do momentarily, let fixity of purpose serve as your guiding light, as you wholly accept that which each moment offers your soul.

Endeavour to always acknowledge your inner power with each stride and be vulnerable enough to let self-love, contentment, and self-belief order your steps as you navigate all of life. May each moment of pain serve as a testament to the strength of your unshakeable spirit, for you are deserving, strong, loved, free, fearless, confident, and creative. You are God, having human expression and experience.

Tomorrow, the apostle's fate will be tried. But this truth does the apostle know: that whatever the outcome, all is in divine hands, for all is well."

"Thank you so much; this moment will never be forgotten," Dr. Ade replied heartily. "These words will I hold sacred. It will serve the purpose it was meant for. Certainly, they will reach the hearts that they are destined for," he assured the apostle.

"My holiday starts tomorrow, and just as you said, all is well no matter the outcome of your tribunal tomorrow. I will take my leave now; do rest well," Dr. Ade said, extending his hand as he shared a handshake with the apostle before leaving the room and closing the door behind him.

MERCENARIES & SALVAGERS

The apostle, in whose eyes knowledge and challenges were bundled, sat with a calm composure in the tribunal room, the atmosphere heavy with unspoken tales. The British-born Sudanese mental health doctor was overly willing to present his case to the tribunal to prove that the apostle's presence had disturbed the peace in the psychiatric facility.

Also seated in the room was the tribunal chairperson, a 6' 2 ft' man in his early fifties from North England. Wearing a fitted blue suit, he sits at the front of the tribunal room, his measured gaze and controlled stance reflecting his years of experience in mental health legislation.

All were seated, waiting for the doctor to present his case and also to assess the mental health status of the apostle and how well he was recuperating based on the up-to-date reports about him. They wanted to determine if he meets the criteria for his sectioning or should be released and maybe leave the hospital. But all indications pointed to the truth that the underhanded management wanted him to leave, as his presence was beginning to threaten their shady agenda.

They aimed to keep patients longer if they remained distressed for financial gain. Disguised as a commitment to extended healing, the agenda sought to exploit insurance reimbursements for profit. Lengthening their therapeutic sessions became a dubious tactic for assuring a steady stream of funds while ignoring the genuine well-being and healing of their patients.

The presence of the apostle, which brought calm and healing to the patients who were being discharged, was a hindrance to the management's achievement of its questionable aims. As a result, his departure was their top priority.

The Chairman of the Tribunal: The purpose of this hearing is to assess the impact of Mr. Apostle's presence in this facility on the mental well-being of the other residents and also to assess the extent to which he has recovered.

Psychiatrist: Your Honour, the holistic well-being of all patients in this hospital is our highest concern and priority, as we all know. The apostle's eccentric behaviour of late, attributed to his diagnosis, is disturbing to the other residents. Though it may be pleasing to the ears and comforting to the soul, your profound musings, Apostle, are causing unease and anxiety among other patients," he said, staring at the apostle, his eyes hiding a dark motive.

The apostle reacted to the allegations and accusations with stoic calm.

Apostle: (With a serene smile on his face) The disturbance, my dear doctor, is but the ripple of a stone falling into the stagnant pond of souls who think that storage is wealth and flow is death. Truly, the patients are disturbed, as they are all part of you.

Threatened by the apostle's profound insights and the things he had heard about him, the tribunal's chairman sought a disguise to silence him.

The chairman of the Tribunal: We are grateful for your fine words, Apostle. You said that you are capable of representing yourself and that you don't need anyone to, so I believe you are capable of making your own decisions. Doc, tell us more about the particular events that led to the formation of this tribunal.

Psychiatrist: Thank you, Your Honour. Many patients have expressed fear, heightened anxiety, and disorientation as a result of the apostle's statements about alternative realms and the delusions he shares. Some of the patients interpret these statements as words of God's wisdom. Two women in the women's ward attacked the staff last night. They believed the staff were giving them poison as a drug to murder them.

The buzzer has been going off in the men's acute ward, and the number of people kicking off has increased. All of this has happened since the apostle was moved to this facility, and it has gotten worse after the talk therapy event. I am sorry to say this, but his presence here is disrupting the therapeutic atmosphere and calm environment we are working hard to create.

The chairman of the tribunal: Mr. Apostle, could you please give your views and perspectives on the allegations against you?

The apostle was silent for a few minutes and broke his silence with a smile. And with a calm expression, he answered thus:

Apostle: Can a prisoner free himself without first struggling with his chains? Can a chick break out of the egg without first breaking the shell? The doctor is right in his assertions. He claims that the other inhabitants are fighting the same battle that has brought us all here at this moment: the fight and the ultimate endeavour to break free.

The mind is a vast universe, and I am a humble wanderer. I share seeds with the soil that are ready to grow trees. I share rain with the seas that are ready to flow. I sell truth like nightmares to slumber heads who have made sleep their purpose of being, so they can wake up and live. These same lights have my friends in this facility tapped into; their souls are now illuminated, and they have seen how thick their chains are. Their struggle and quest to set themselves free have been called disturbances.

Are you not also a patient? Have you not tapped into the same light? Has your soul not been enlightened, and is your wrongdoing not visible like golden leaves on fig trees in the fall? "What dark truths must dwell within you, that in the brilliance of light, your actions reveal such hideousness? What drives you to extinguish that radiant glow or shatter the mirror that so boldly reveals your true reflection?"

Psychiatrist: These confusing and illusory tales are what I mean, sir. His stories lead to nothing but confusion and anxiety in other patients. They lead to anger and tension among the patients in the men's ward. This is one thing we cannot and mustn't compromise on at this time. The inconsiderate behaviour of the residents and its impact on the staff has already begun to cast a negative light on us as a psychiatric facility.

Two members of staff have already handed in their resignation notices due to the consequences of the attack on the night staff a few days ago. If nothing is done and the situation escalates, it'll be embarrassing that we knew what to do but didn't do it. That would be a breach of ethical mental healthcare laws and safeguarding regulations.

Apostle: (With a soft laugh) Truth causes internal disturbances before it heals, doctor; doesn't the builder scatter before they build? Why are you concerned about their disturbances? Isn't healing the reason they are here?

Verily, awakening is a stormy journey, but essential.

Tribunal Chairman: Doctor, you have heard the apostle. So, how do you intend to deal with the present situation?

Psychiatrist: Our job in this hospital is to create a stable and healing environment. That cannot be changed because of one individual. We cannot jeopardise the health of so many vulnerable residents in these wards because of one man. Our main goal is to promote rapid recovery and healing. And by all indications, the apostle's unusual stories could thwart that goal.

Apostle: Once again, I ask you, Doc, is it healing you seek? Healing, my friend, is not always a silent stream. No river flows quietly; to flow is to heal. If healing is what you seek, then be still, for storms awaken the soul, not destroy it. What charm does fire have if it does not burn? What beauty does truth have if it does not awaken God from his slumber? If you strive for gain and possessions, then make room for sorrow in your soul, for it will dwell majestically within it.

A wave of silence swept through the room. The contrast between conventional psychiatry, the doctor's subliminal intention, and the apostle's esoteric insights all hung in the air.

Tribunal Chairman: Apostle, the truth is that I may not understand everything you have just said. Based on your current reputation in the ward, I firmly believe that your wisdom is evident, but we must consider the overall impact on the residents. Can you assure us that your discussions will not disturb the peace and serenity of this facility?

Apostle: (pausing) I can promise only that my intent is pure. Only this can the apostle control. Abdul Malik is but a vessel, sharing the echoes of existence that exist in the corridors of the mind. Does the vessel have control over the water that flows from it and drops to the floor if the water sweeps people off their feet? The vessel can only promise to do its work, to be empty enough to always be full of light, and to be full enough to never think it will ever run empty from shining.

The Tribunal Chairman: Who is Abdul Malik, if I may ask? (He stares sternly at the apostle.). I really can't comprehend who Adul Malik is. Or is that your name? Doctor, I am confused (He stares at the doctor).

Psychiatrist: That's exactly what I was talking about— the delusional and Barmecidal speeches. As far as we know, he said his name was Apostle, and that's all we know about him, in all honesty.

Apostle: (stares at them with a grin on his face, without saying a word.).

The Tribunal Chairman: Doctor, what are your thoughts? Do you think a middle ground can be reached here?

Psychiatrist: Perhaps we could set up observed conversations in a particular place to reduce the overall impact on the inhabitants, while also increasing his observations. Essentially, this will only work if the decision is for him to stay, and I don't think that will happen. I want to avoid making a compromise that could jeopardise the safety and well-being of the other residents.

Apostle: (Interrupting) Can truth be hidden or life tamed? Can observations on your soul be increased or are your thoughts watched? Is Abdul Malik not a mirror for your soul? Will breaking the mirror for not loving what it serves you in the form of your reflection break your reflection?

How narcissistic is your soul!

You destroy the soul because you can't destroy the light, and it reveals all that you hide in the dark. Oh, ye ego-driven mercenaries! Because you can't destroy your reflection, you destroy the mirror. Hasn't that been your sign of life? Are all aspects of life, not mirrors? Is Abdul Malik not a reflection of life itself, with his words serving as a mirror to our souls? Suppress it with ideas, control its words with laws and rules, and bind its hands with conventions and trends. Verily, the mirror can be destroyed, but the reflection will remain.

But how many mirrors can you destroy? How many salvagers can you hold captive? How much of life can you tame? How much suppression can your soul endure? Is Abdul Malik not a resident of your soul? How many of its words can you monitor?

How much of its observation can you amplify?

The psychiatrist's expression grew tense, a flicker of irritation in his eyes as the apostle spoke truths that challenged their agenda. The tribunal's chair, once quiet, shifted uneasily. His forced smile and fake grin were suddenly strained, betraying the discomfort hidden behind his creative and carefully forged façade.

The Tribunal Chairman: We appreciate your distinct point of view and its potential benefits, Apostle. However, we need to strike a balance.

Doc," He said, staring at the doctor, "I suggest we adopt your mitigation plan. By instituting supervised conversations in a designated area, we can accommodate both the apostle's therapeutic needs and his desire to share his thoughts.

What do you think, Apostle? (He stared at the Apostle, waiting for him to speak.).

Apostle: Once again, I implore you, as I have always done with your fathers. The words of Abdul Malik are mirrors reflecting the truth within you that you try so hard to hide. Your mitigation plan for damage control is characterised by the fear of your secret intentions being exposed, hence your desire to expel the apostle.

The apostle does no harm; rather, he serves as a catalyst for awakening. When you try to drive it away, you deny souls the elixir of knowledge. My presence is a light on the path of all passengers in eternity. Your fear stains the canvas on which this moment is so beautifully painted, but my purpose transcends the limits you impose upon me. Aye, buried in your rapacious intent to silence wisdom, you amplify the echoes of truth.

All is well, and the apostle is at peace, for he is but a passenger in eternity. If he chooses freedom, then his purpose will be stifled. Verily, the time has come for the apostle to be on his way again; his time here is thus done. The apostle will make a heartfelt decision to leave.

The Tribunal Chairman: (looking at the apostle) Don't you think you should reconsider this decision? I understand everything you have said, and I suggest you think about it a little more before you make your final decision. Our top priority here is to make sure that you receive the best care and support that this facility can provide, so that when you return to the community, you can express and experience life like everyone else.

Our plan has never been to prevent you from expressing yourself; that is your right, and we cannot take that away from you. Any attempt to do so would be a bad practice that goes against the ethics of care. We simply want to create a harmonious and calm environment in the facility that contributes to the healing and holistic well-being of you and other residents.

With this in mind, we will take a ten-minute coffee break to give you time to think things over before you decide whether you want to go or stay.

Apostle: There is no reason for the break, for the appointed time is now. I will pack up my things and take my leave. This palace was a wonderful place for the apostle to pitch his tent and empty himself. He has thus emptied himself for the souls who needed his light. For those sailing through the stormy seas, his energy has become a beacon of light that softens their sails. The apostle regrets nothing, for he has done nothing that is not in harmony with what is.

The apostle's decision echoed through the tribunal room. The psychiatrist, with an apologetic demeanour, uttered words of apology over the old sage's decision to leave.

Psychiatrist: Are you sure about this decision, Apostle? I sincerely agree with what the chairman said. I think you should take your time and think it through. We all love your presence and would like you to stay and be cared for by the doctors and staff here. You just need to compromise a little so that the place can be conducive for you and the other residents. Don't you think that can be achieved?

Apostle: The apostle, like air, cannot be contained inside this building's enormous walls. The soul knows that severity comes when the leaves turn golden. My leaves are thus golden, even though fall is nowhere near.

What is the point of reaching a compromise when your world demands conformity and mine craves everlasting understanding?

I live to share truths, not to destroy them. When I take my leave, I leave you a torch with which to examine your souls and fill the void of emptiness within you. My existence in this facility may be extinguished by this institution, but the echo of Abdul Malik will live on in your hearts for all eternity, guiding those who want more from life as they experience and express more than what you have to offer, and reminding those who have forgotten who they truly are.

Tribunal Chair: We'd like to conclude by acknowledging your decision to leave, and we wish you luck on the next phase of your journey. The council will collaborate with this organisation to find a suitable location for your ongoing care, support, and progress, since they are aware of your unique needs.

As we bid farewell, may you find solace in environments that value your profound knowledge and insightful opinions. Being a premier mental health organisation, our commitment to patient-centred care extends beyond these walls. Thus, the doctors will make sure you receive regular checkups and the support you need. I appreciate your time and wish that the words of wisdom you share find a suitable place to blossom.

For safeguarding reasons, you will not return to the ward for the time being. Therefore, we have provided a room outside the building where you can spend the rest of the day until the Council arrives tomorrow and takes you to the place where you are to be housed.

The staff will collect your belongings and send them to the place where you will be temporarily accommodated.

Psychiatrist: Thank you for your time, Apostle. Do you have any questions about the Tribunal chairman's decision?

Apostle: (with a grin on his face) All is indeed well. My regards to everyone; they all made my journey what it was meant to be. What purpose would the tongue serve if the heart were numb to its words? My regards also go to Doctor Ade; it is a pity I couldn't bid him a grand farewell, but the words of Abdul Malik are forever young in the hearts of those who are intimate with life itself.

Psychiatrist: (With a sardonic look on his face) They will surely hear. We will make sure your farewell message gets through to everyone. Thank you again for your time, Apostle; we will truly miss you.

They all stood up, the tribunal chairman packed up the files on the table, and the psychiatrist cleared away the disposable cups on the table and adjusted his belt.

The apostle walked quietly to the door, closely followed by two members of staff who escorted him out of the building and towards an apartment near the facility, where he would spend the rest of the day before being taken by the council to his new home.

Note To Self

Blind eyes see the most beautiful things

Lame legs walk the most adorned roads.

Dumb tongues speak the most heartfelt words.

Clogged nostrils value breath the most.

Pure hearts feel the best of grief.

Sad minds come alive in misery; they steal joy like thieves.

Heavy heads record the most dreams

Lazy hands and a dead will create sad endings, it seems

Their mouths and bellies are filled with sad tales of would-haves and should-haves

But on each other's shoulders, they unceasingly lean.

Curious Minds row their boats gently

For Life is but a dream.

A bad day is the most suitable title for expectations not lived.

The hunting melody of sorrows that weary souls sing

But in all divine art and acts of creation,

Deadbeat dads and masculine mums

seem to create the most traumatised kids.

Silver tears are the best expression for golden joys

Silence is the loudest noise for avoidant souls

Love is the softest song that cracks thick walls

And pain is the most beautiful thing living things share in common.

About the Author

Born amidst the rich contrasts of eastern Nigeria, I was shaped not by silence, but by noise—the kind that stirs a mind into motion. As a child, I rarely sat still. While others walked straight paths, I traced patterns in the margins, drawn to the unseen, the unspoken, the unresolved.

There was always something stirring just beneath the surface—questions that refused easy answers, emotions I couldn't name but instinctively felt, and a world that moved too slowly for the pulse in my head. I wasn't rebellious; I just danced to a rhythm others couldn't hear. And when the world misunderstood that rhythm, I retreated—not to escape, but to listen more closely.

In solitude, I found language. In stillness, I found depth. I turned inward not as a form of withdrawal, but as an act of discovery. From there, my obsession with the human psyche emerged—not as a subject to master, but as a mirror to experience.

That journey led me into the labyrinth of psychology, not to fix what's broken, but to guide others through the wild terrain of their inner lives. My work doesn't follow a straight line. It spirals, echoes, and returns to the same place with new eyes. Whether through soul therapy, writing, or creative direction, I aim to stir something that's already within—the quiet knowing, the seed of transformation.

Now based in the UK, I blend spiritual inquiry with psychotherapeutic insight, philosophical thought with visceral art. I call this healing from the inside out. Some call me The Mind Surgeon. I call myself an experiencer—of patterns, of meaning, of the idea of self.

Through this Work Of Art, I offer not answers but invitations—to slow down, look within, and meet yourself at the edge of becoming.

Victor Kwesi

Printed and bound by CPI Group (UK) Ltd, Croydon, CR0 4YY
04/08/2025
01930265-0001